Praise for

The Graduate Business Own

T0272847

"If you want to be in the driver's seat of your business this book is a must-read. It will help you identify, plan, and execute your chosen path to success regardless of your business stage."

John Rainey
Director (retired), Clark University Small Business Development Center

The Graduate Level of Business Ownership is a must-read for any current or aspiring business owner. It is a down-to-earth compilation of sage wisdom, extensive experience, and practical advice which will rigorously inform the reader in all facets of business ownership. I personally value the blending of business advice with the psychological dynamics at play in Shefer and Shepherd's approach. The use of real-world examples also allows us to take a deep dive into stories that are current, relevant, and relatable. What lingers most is that the "graduate level of ownership" is primarily about enjoying the journey along the way, a concept worth remembering and living.

Cynthia Adams Harrison, Ed. D., LICSW
Elite Performance Coaching for Business, Sport and Life

Few books provide their readers with a graduate degree. An easy read, this book does so succinctly with the right amount of anecdotes. Shefer and Shepherd provide a road map for business owners to get their "degree" by running their business like investors, giving them the confidence that the business can run well without their direct engagement and, in doing so, increase the value of their business. It comes down to goal setting, follow-through, and then some letting go.

Chris Mellen
Senior Managing Director, Valuation Research Corporation
Author, Valuation for M&A: Building and Measuring Private Company Value

After more than forty years of searching to find what works and what doesn't for private business owners, Terry and Ronen have captured the very best! As experienced professionals, their strategic insights and use of tools like the Value Gap and What-If analysis will surely help owners and advisors plan to get the most from what they got! Congratulations, Terry and Ronen, and thank you for sharing this valuable know-how.

Michael R. Nall
Cofounder, MidMarket Alliance
Founder, Alliance of M&A Advisors

For those working in their business on a day-to-day basis, improving the enterprise, strengthening management, and eventually selling the business or transferring ownership to the next generation involves a difficult journey, one that few of us have experience with. In *The Graduate Level of Business Ownership*, Terry Shepherd and Ronen Shefer act as guides, putting into clear terms what the process looks like, as well as outlining the many stumbling blocks there are along the way. Filled with stories and anecdotes, you are sure to see your situation, thoughts, and concerns reflected in these pages. As a client, I have found the ROCG methodology to be a valuable road map—from the initial stages that focus on building value in the enterprise through all the ensuing steps in executing a successful transition. As a business-to-business publisher and event organizer, I'm a true believer in the advice laid out in this book. It's an invaluable resource for any business owner who needs to navigate the path from ownership to the next stage of their life and career, no matter where they are on that journey.

Peter Stanton
CEO & Publisher, New England Business Media LLC

The Graduate Level of Business Ownership covers the whole spectrum of creating a successful plan for business and personal success. The authors have decades of real-life experiences, with hundreds of business owner clients in various stages of growth and maturity. The actual examples they share bring all the concepts to life. That kind of expertise is priceless, and they've laid it out for the benefit of anyone who is open to learning what they don't know. This is a must-read for any small business owner.

Kenneth J. Sanginario, CVGA, CM&AA, CTP, ABV, MST, MSF
Founder, Corporate Value Metrics

Terry and Ronen, I want to sincerely thank you and your organization for the invaluable advice you have given me and my family in counseling and transitioning our business to the next level. The end result was transformative. Fortunately, I was introduced to you at a critical time and you were instrumental in transitioning myself and my family to a new reality. The process was not easy, and it took a lot of energy and focus to resolve. In the end, the advice and input you gave was consistent, pointed, and matter-of-fact. Without your knowledge and advice, we would never have achieved the exceptional outcome that we realized. I truly believe in the process and outcomes that you have shared in your book, and I know that anyone that reads and employs the advice delineated in this book will be greatly rewarded.

Craig Bovaird

Former owner and CEO, Reliance Engineering; Built-Rite Tool & Die Inc.

Anyone thinking of starting, running, or selling their own business should read this book. For each phase of a business life cycle, *The Graduate Level of Business Ownership* lays out the structural steps that are necessary for success and addresses the emotions that come with the journey. On all accounts it is a real-world road map for success—and I should know, since my true story is highlighted in the book!

Dennis A. (a.k.a. Daniel)

Owner, TechnoWorks, Inc.

THE
Graduate Level
OF Business
Ownership

The Secrets to Business Success and Personal Happiness

RONEN SHEFER · TERENCE J. SHEPHERD

Advantage | Books

Published by Advantage, Charleston, South Carolina.
Member of Advantage Media Group.

ADVANTAGE is a registered trademark, and the Advantage colophon is a trademark of Advantage Media Group, Inc.

Printed in the United States of America.

10 9 8 7 6 5 4 3 2 1

ISBN: 978-1-64225-538-6 (Paperback)
ISBN: 978-1-64225-537-9 (eBook)

LCCN: 2022915065

Cover design by Analisa Smith.
Layout design by Wesley Strickland.

This publication is designed to provide accurate and authoritative information in regard to the subject matter covered. It is sold with the understanding that the publisher is not engaged in rendering legal, accounting, or other professional services. If legal advice or other expert assistance is required, the services of a competent professional person should be sought.

Advantage Media Group is a publisher of business, self-improvement, and professional development books and online learning. We help entrepreneurs, business leaders, and professionals share their Stories, Passion, and Knowledge to help others Learn & Grow. Do you have a manuscript or book idea that you would like us to consider for publishing? Please visit **advantagefamily.com**.

Terence

To my two "little" angel girls, Caroline and Nora—you were indeed a precious gift to me and Mom by the grace of God.

And to my wife Catherine, who changed my life for the better and who has always stood by my side through the highs and lows of our life's journey.

I am so blessed to have the three of you in my life. I love you to the moon and back.

Ronen

For most of us, life's journey begins with parents or caretakers who help shape who we end up becoming. So I want to start by dedicating this book to my parents, Michael and Caspit, whose individual stories deserve a book of their own.

To my wife Teresa, without whom this project would have likely never happened. Thank you for sharing this wonderful life journey with me and for always supporting my craziest ideas, all while you continue your own efforts to make this world a better place. I love you honey!

And finally to my kids, Trevor and Miah. I'm glad you did not follow in our footsteps and instead created your own paths. I hope you always remember this: "Good things may come to those who wait, but they come a lot sooner if you simply go and get them!" I'm proud of you both!

Contents

ACKNOWLEDGMENTS

T his project, several years in the making, could not have been accomplished without the help of many people and organizations. First, we simply want to acknowledge all those who came before us with their books and perspectives, and especially those who we quoted or referenced in the book. With this book, we seek to continue to carry the torch, to convince more business owners to incorporate life planning and business planning on a road to a more fulfilling life journey.

Second, we want to acknowledge our advisor on this project, Gary Lee, who was indefatigably patient as we worked and reworked through numerous revisions, and without whom this project would have never been completed.

We also want to thank our ROCG partners and industry friends, some of whom we have known for over three decades, who took part in developing and finetuning some of our consultative processes, systems, and best practices, and whose support made this book possible.

Finally, we want to acknowledge and thank all the business owners we have had the pleasure to work with over the years—not just the ones highlighted in this book. Even though they came to us for help, they are an inspiration to us in their willingness to risk everything to build something that can support so many other families in the community. We hope they inspire the next generations of business owners and leaders!

We want to give special acknowledgement to a few people: Bruce Wright, an early pioneer in the business and personal transition space on how business owners should align their business strategy with their personal goals and objectives; Richard Jackim and Peter Christman, who identified the needs of business owners and the opportunity for professionals in the business transition and value growth space with their book, *The $10 Trillion Opportunity*; and finally the Alliance of Merger and Acquisition Advisors and their founder and prior longtime president, Michael Nall, who provided the platform to share current practices, connect to a large group of M&A professionals to collaborate on insights, and provide a continuous learning opportunity throughout the country and beyond.

PREFACE

We wrote this book hoping to inspire business owners to align their business aspirations with their personal lives. In other words, we want to motivate owners to view their journey through life not only from the point of view of the business and its successes or failures, but to also focus on defining life objectives so they can ultimately use the business as the catalyst to help them achieve those objectives.

We also want owners to learn best practices in running a successful business, take the steps to ensure they start living a more fulfilling life, and eventually transition from daily hands-on management to the Graduate Level of Business Ownership.

In our work with hundreds of small- and medium-sized and family-owned businesses, we saw an unfulfilled need in the marketplace. In this book, we seek to respond to that need by sharing our proven processes and insight to hopefully help more business owners get control of their business, get control of their personal lives, become more profitable, build greater value, and start living the life they want.

We start with the right way to create and think about the business, proceed with how to grow it and make sure it is not dependent on the owner, and continue with the ways they can live a well-balanced life, finally leading up to the possibility of exiting the business on their terms and timetable.

As a society, we often evaluate a business's success by how big or profitable it is or how much money it can be sold for. The reality is much simpler. It boils down to whether business owners can live their dreams and fulfill their life objectives. Those are the ultimate success criteria for any owner.

CHAPTER ONE

What If There's No Tomorrow?

The Case for Business and Life Planning

T om's life is strikingly similar to that of most small business owners. In his early sixties, he is the sole owner of a machine parts business that he has owned for two decades. Jane, his wife, manages their household and occasionally assists with the business's administrative functions. The couple has been married for thirty-five years. They have two adult sons, Max and Adam.

Both work as managers in the company.

Throughout their history of business ownership, Tom and Jane's life together has been regimented and uneventful, especially as of late. They normally wake up together at about 6:00 a.m. Tom leaves at 7:00 a.m. to open the shop. They tend to have at least one phone call midday, and Tom tries to return home about 6:00 p.m. in time for dinner before doing some additional work at his home office. But today was different. Tom had just arrived home from work, and as they began to sit down for dinner, Jane asked, "Did you hear the news about Phil?"

For years, Phil had been a neighbor and a fellow business owner. A couple of years back, he sold his successful software company and moved his family to Florida.

"What happened?" Tom asked.

Jane stared somberly. "He died."

She then shared the full story, which she had learned earlier that day in a call with Phil's wife. After the business sale and relocation, Phil had been at a loss as to what to do with his time. He had devoted his life to the business. That was all he knew. Without it, he fell into a depression. That, in turn, precipitated illness and his premature demise.

"Jane, what?" Tom replied. "Are you sure? He seemed so happy. It doesn't make sense!" he added.

The news shocked Tom. He compared himself to Phil. He viewed their work and life situations as similar. Both were around the same age, parents and grandparents, owners closely engaged with their businesses. Tom knew that Phil had gotten a good offer, and the sale of the business had happened quickly. There hadn't been much time for planning. Still, Tom had envied Phil's retirement. Now he was gone. Tom couldn't help but think, *This could easily happen to me. I have not done any planning either. I too could die without much of a plan to protect my family or the business. And, without a plan for how to spend the rest of my life, I could see myself falling into the same cycle of depression and demise that Phil suffered.*

Throughout dinner and afterward, a rush of questions and thoughts raced through his mind.

What will happen to my family if I fall ill or die? While Phil died after selling the business, the thoughts of Tom's own mortality were front and center for him all evening. For the past two decades, he had devoted all his energy and time to making his business a success. Now almost all his wealth was tied up in it. It had certainly provided him and his family a good lifestyle, but was there enough value in the business to meet his future lifestyle objectives after a sale? Tom knew that he needed to focus on the future and funding his retirement years—but at the very least he needed to have a plan in place that protected his wife and family, something that would allow them to live well in case something unexpected happened to him. But knowing you need to do something and actually doing it are two separate things. Where would he begin? Tom was lost.

How can I make sure the business is passed on to the next generation and continues to thrive without me? After twenty years, Tom's business still does not have an exit plan or contingency plan. He would like for the business to stay in the family. But he doesn't know how to reconcile the rivalry between Max and Adam, his sons. Both have ambitions to run the business one day.

What can I do to have a fulfilling life while I am still running the company and the years afterward? For Tom, the biggest takeaway from Phil's fate was that he needed to work on his own goals, objectives, and legacy. His days—and many evenings—were consumed by the business. Now the company is financially stable. He needs to find a way to eventually cash out and monetize all of his hard work during the last twenty years. Beyond that, he has to have a plan for that next phase of his life, so his time is occupied with something fulfilling, something that keeps him from suffering the same fate as Phil. What he yearns for is more personal time—the opportunity to do some volunteer work, read, travel, and, most importantly, spend more time with his family. In this moment of honesty, he acknowledges that there's room for improvement in his marriage. He can also be a better parent to Max and Adam and a better grandfather to their children.

Would coping with a transition be easier or more complicated if I had a business partner? Tom had been approached several times by other business owners to form a partnership. After careful thought, he had opted against it. Now he wondered if dealing with issues such as legacy and transition would be easier or more complex if he had a partner to share the responsibilities of ownership.

None of these questions was new to Tom. One or another of them had been on his mind for years. But the demands of the business did not allow time to focus on them, let alone make decisions. Instead, he kept putting off dealing with them until some undefined time in the future. After all, he thought, there was always tomorrow to work on it. The news about Phil forced him to see things from a different perspective. He now had to consider something he had never thought about: What if there is no tomorrow?

The story of Tom, Jane, and Phil is a parable. But the questions and points it raises are real. All of Tom's issues—contingency planning, ensuring the business provides enough value to fund his future lifestyle objectives, whether or how to transition or exit, how to create a legacy, fulfilling responsibilities to family and other special people—are things every business owner should address at some stage. Tom's thoughts about a partnership are real too. Business owners with one or multiple partners have similar questions to Tom's, multiplied by several times as the need of each owner differs. As a result, many sole business owners debate the pros and cons of partnership particularly when they reach a crossroads.

Tom's approach to the dilemmas he posed also rings true. Like him, many owners avoid contingency planning, life planning, and strategic planning, particularly if they involve emotional subjects. They hope the issues will resolve themselves. Instead, they focus on the day-to-day demands of their businesses. The reasons are understandable. In Tom's business—like most—there seems to be a fire every day. And fires, as every business owner knows, have to be dealt with right away. Issues like legacy planning seem far away, things that can be done some other time down the road. It's a line of thinking based on the misguided mindset that there will always be a tomorrow.

> *It is our belief that owners should organize the planning and running of their businesses to incorporate the demands of their business lives and personal lives at the same time.*

It is our belief that owners should organize the planning and running of their businesses to incorporate the demands of their business lives and personal lives at the same time and gradually build the business so that it works for them rather than them working for it.

The Fear of Tackling Tough Issues

As business exit and value growth specialists who have worked with hundreds of clients, we have found that fear is the major barrier keeping many business owners from dealing with topics like their life objectives, business planning, or ultimately transitioning out of the business. Owners' fears are wide ranging. For some, the biggest fear is of the unknown. For a business owner who has been in control, not knowing what comes next is very frightening. For others, it's a fear of risking the investment and ongoing cash flow they have devoted much of their lives to building up. And when it comes to exiting out of the company one day, some fear the possible loss of identity after no longer being part of something they were associated closely with for years or, in many cases, decades. "I like being known as the car guy," as one owner put it. What will I be known as now? The retired guy?"

To many business owners, these fears are rooted in a feeling that any transition means leaving something behind. And it's not just anything they think they're leaving. The business in most cases is a comfort zone, something they have invested in heavily. In essence, it's their baby. But that thought process is also the main barrier preventing many owners from reaching the graduate level of business ownership. Rather than dwelling on the potential of leaving something behind, we encourage business owners to view any business initiative, including transitioning their responsibilities or selling the business one day, as a move to the next phase of their lives that includes something positive to walk toward.

Particularly for those who have devoted a big part of their lives to the demands of business ownership, we encourage the process of discovery or the uncovering of personal passions and values that bring them their greatest enjoyment and discerning what things would be nice to have versus the things that they are truly committed to going after. The focus should be on creating goals and activities that bring personal meaning to their life. Often that active search for meaning motivates business owners to think enthusiastically about what they want to accomplish in their lives while still running the business but especially in the postbusiness ownership phase of their lives.

No matter how challenging a decision, similar to an owner's personal savings and investment planning, the longer business owners have to implement and execute their plan, the better the results will be and the better chance they have of meeting their goals successfully. That's not to say that the decisions will be easy. Whether they are about creating a contingency plan, engaging family in the business, or something else, the considerations are often complex. That alone causes many business owners to put off planning. But they shouldn't. An experienced advisor with the right expertise can break down the complexities into manageable components.

Key Factors in Planning and Executing Are Often Ignored

Even for owners in the initial phase of exploring their eventual exit or transition—never mind those with a fifteen to twenty years' time horizon—operating the business at the graduate level makes all the difference in the world of being able to achieve business success and personal happiness. As stated above, for us it often starts by helping owners discover those things most important to them and assisting them in identifying goals and objectives that will best bring them the greatest fulfillment and joy—a life plan per se. For example: Do they have things they always wanted to do but never got a chance to do? Are there personal financial objectives they hope to achieve? Do they have a major scaling mindset that will take years to fulfill? Do they want to maintain ownership for a few more years and then start transitioning to the next phase of their lives? Or is the plan to keep the business in the family and pass ownership to other family members at some point? Do they want to maintain a role in the company after a transition?

There are many questions to explore, and these are just a small sample of the kinds of questions we pose to engage owners. What you will notice immediately is that this type of planning is not solely focused on the business's growth, unit sales cost, or other operating metrics. It begins first and foremost with the owner and his or her significant other's goals, objectives, and value drivers. Only after identifying their personal life objectives, do we begin working with them using the business as the catalyst to achieve them.

At the heart of this, is the realization by business owners that from the first day they start their enterprise, someday they will leave the business. The only question is whether the owner will be walking out the door on their own two feet or going out feet first. It will all come down to whether a business owner takes the time to plan and prepare in order to fulfill life goals and have minimal regrets when it's all said and done.

With various factors coming into play, both business and transition plans are all unique to each person and circumstance. But underneath it all, the process of creating and executing a successful holistic plan, and the secrets of most successful business owners, are all based on these four constant factors.

First, establishing, maintaining, and building on the financial success of the business within a specific timetable is key. Establishing goals helps drive decisions about how to build the business's value, reduce the dependency on the owner, and determine the personal planning action steps that may be integral to the overall plan. Higher profitability and a higher overall business value will help the owner or owners meet their current and future lifestyle objectives. It will also help ensure that the business is on an upward growth and profitability track at the time of the exit—something a sophisticated buyer will be seeking.

Second, recognizing and addressing the right-brain or emotional issues is paramount.

Because our recommendation for these business plans is to link them back to personal objectives, during this process, we try to identify any emotional restraints that may hold the owner back. We do so because many plans go off track or are halted altogether because of unidentified emotional issues that surface during the plans' execution. Those issues, we have found, are often rooted in the owner's personal dilemmas. Owners need to keep in mind that business and life planning are not all about the money and left-brain analytics. Therefore, successful business owners learn how to address these issues head on and not ignore them.

They can be the difference between a successful and joyful life journey, or one filled with regrets.

Third, allowing enough time to successfully execute a plan that meets an owner's goals and objectives is also key. Unfortunately, many business owners operate under the impressions that implementing change can be accomplished within a short time period, and exiting their business is a quick, one-time event. When they are ready to execute—for example in the case of selling their business—they often think they will simply put the business up for sale and then move on, hoping that the sale yields enough. They don't bother to calculate how long the sale proceeds will last given their lifestyle spending needs or consider what they will do next—what activity will fill their time and be fulfilling. A successful plan is a process; the more time a business owner spends planning that process and putting it into action, the better.

Fourth, be warned that strategic business plans typically fail. Study after study shows that lack of execution is the main reason. So, for value growth planning, life planning, and an eventual exit to succeed, business owners must commit to its diligent execution over the long haul. Business owners have plenty of stories of ideas and strategies that didn't work for one reason or another. The successful outcome occurs more times than not for owners who are persistent and don't give up when things don't go exactly right or expected outcomes take longer than originally expected. Instead, they learn over time that there is no silver bullet for immediate success. While the business concepts are easy to understand, it's the execution that's the hard part. It takes tenacity to see things through to a successful outcome.

John, a sole owner of a chain of car dealerships, is a good example of how these factors come into play in discussions about planning an eventual business transition. John owned his business for eighteen years. He'd been divorced for five years. Since the divorce, he had begun withdrawing more money from the business and devoting more time to his personal life. He also had a goal of selling his business in ten years.

Having an objective and a time frame for reaching it were positive steps. But John had no plan for how he would get there, and he had not identified the value gap between the current value of his business and his goal. The business was not creating sufficient profit to sustain either his current or future lifestyle.

As part of our standard planning process, which we will detail later in the book, we explored John's plan and engaged him in a discussion of emotional issues he was facing. In his case, a major issue was that he had come to use the business as a piggy bank for years and could not see it any other way. He drew directly from the business's operating profits to support his lavish lifestyle, sometimes taking out tens of thousands of dollars on a regular basis. The emotional aspect of this habit centered on his tendency to act independently and commingle personal money and business money. This strategy might have been smart if John had invested the money and by doing so diversified his holdings from his business to several other investments—in essence, taking some chips off the table. But he was using the funds to pay for expensive vacations, luxury cars, and other personal items. With the majority of their wealth tied up in the business, there is often a tradeoff that is needed between the amount owners need to support a comfortable lifestyle and what they need to put away to fund retirement savings.

John was eventually able to come to terms with the reasons behind his habit. At its core, John not only thought that he deserved the lavish lifestyle as a reward for his hard work, but his circle of friends almost forced this lifestyle on him as a way to simply keep up with them. Once John understood these drivers and was able to reflect on the long-term ramifications of his behavior, he was better able to separate business money from personal money.

That, in turn, helped him create his transition plan. John's willingness to consider the four factors we outlined above were crucial in his ability to move ahead: he made a commitment to work on a plan, and he was honest about the emotional issues involved. He also gave himself a good amount of time to meet all of his financial and nonfinancial objectives, and he took advantage of building on the business's success with a specific time frame for action.

Leaving the Business One Day Is Inevitable

Not many business owners take the initial steps that John did—to consider transition or contingency planning early enough. More often, they may call in an advisor only after some sudden life-changing event occurs. For many owners, like Tom—the character in the opening scene of this chapter—it takes being hit with a sudden death, illness, or other crisis for them to understand how important it is to have a plan in place. When a dramatic event such as a death or serious illness happens, the options for working out a solution are far more limited.

Donald is a good case in point. He was an eighty-three-year-old owner of a software company with around eighty employees. He had kept tight control of his business, made all decisions, and didn't build a strong management team that could step in and take over.

> *It takes being hit with a sudden death, illness, or some other crisis for business owners to understand how important it is to have a plan in place.*

Although the company had been successful, the revenues had begun to fall. Then Donald had an auto accident, caused by a health complication. Lacking any contingency plan, he was persuaded that he needed to seek help creating a transition plan. Through a referral, he came to us for help.

In our talks with Donald and other employees, several issues facing the company emerged. After the accident, many of the senior employees were worried and fearful about their job security. Some had already left for the competition, and others were poised to depart. Neither of Donald's sons was prepared to take over the business, for different reasons.

This was a case where it was crucial for the owner to face his/her own health problems and their consequences for the business. The full range of emotional issues that many business owners must face came into full play: how to deal with mortality; how to secure what you have worked for after you are gone; how your family will be cared for.

Time was not on our side. Donald's age and health issues gave an urgency to structuring a viable transition plan. And the imminent retirement of a couple of senior managers only added to the urgency.

Even in cases without those added constraints, the more time allowed to come up with a plan, the better. If Donald had taken the time to plan before he was forced to, he could have exercised control and put things in place to maintain the community commitment and work environment that were important to him. He could also have protected the long-time employees by allowing them to continue to work after he sold, giving them a place to go in an effort to give them purpose.

In the end, we held a series of meetings with trusted managers and other employees and arrived at a transition plan. Fortunately, Don had a nephew that previously worked in the business who also owned his own business. So he had an understanding of the business, knew some of the senior employees, and had experience running a successful company. They all knew the nephew and felt better for the long-term sustainability of the company having him on board. While not ideal, it was a plan that Donald and the senior managers could accept without the luxury of time to seek alternative options.

The Search for Life's Meaning

When business owners—like most people—begin to consider what is most important in their lives, their thoughts turn to life's meaning and purpose, and oftentimes their attention is directed to forging closer family bonds. In many cases, over the years, business owners have sacrificed time with their families to meet the demands of the business. The process of recouping lost family time or shoring up relations with a spouse, children, or grandchildren is usually wrought with emotions. Business owners tend to be aware of the challenge but unsure how to address it.

That search for meaning is never easy. It requires business owners to tap into emotional areas that many are not used to exploring or are comfortable with. When owners are earnest and diligent in this pursuit, it leads to surprising discoveries. When they are rushed or not fully engaged, the process can easily fall short of the goal.

One case that comes to mind involved Bryan, a business owner in his late seventies; his wife, Lillian; and their middle-aged son, Junior. Bryan started his business career from scratch and went on a mission to amass as much wealth as possible. It was a goal he met. He eventually owned multiple businesses, all of them successful. By all accounts he was a brilliant business owner. And he and his son were a great team.

But the success came because he was always on and all business. To Bryan, the tendency for hands-on tight control was ingrained and as natural as breathing. He did not know how to let go. Unfortunately for his family, he was the same at home as at work.

Bryan reached out to us to discuss transition planning. How could he forge a deal with his son to take over the business? But he had another, more personal objective. When questioned about what he ultimately wanted, he said, "All I want is for Junior to say he loves me." For him, that simple emotional expression from his offspring would be the greatest possible return on investment he could get from the years of work he had put into business ownership. That moment hit us like a ton of bricks. How very sad. Here was a very successful businessman who took no time to develop a life plan, who now in the latter part of his life was searching for purpose and found himself living a life of regret.

We had several key meetings with Bryan, his wife, and their son. Bryan's overbearing character, coupled with unresolved issues in the family, created an atmosphere of tension in the meetings. Bryan's failing health put us on a short time frame. His son was very competent and ran large parts of the operations already. But to meet Bryan's wishes, he would have to shift more of the business's final decision-making responsibilities to his son. That was a very hard thing for him to do. The fear of lack of control and the loss of wealth held him back. He would also have to take time away from the business and slowly get involved in the personal lives of his three children, including Junior, and his grandchildren. That too was very difficult for him and would require him to change his priorities in order to take part in their personal lives. He would need to learn empathetic supportive personal communication skills, all of which would take tremendous effort over a long period of time. What this owner wanted as the end goal of his transition and exit plan was fraught with challenges. If a successful resolution was possible, it could only be achieved by a sustained, long-term commitment—something, regrettably, the owner no longer had. Although Bryan and Lillian thought they were making some progress after each meeting, there were too many challenges and not enough time to resolve them. We parted ways as a result.

Keeping the family abreast or even engaging them in the business is also something that can never start too early. We've seen too many cases where a family is left with a business they have very little knowledge about. No one better illustrates this scenario than Sam, a longtime owner of a menswear business. Like most owners he had not considered transition planning previously. But he came to us one day with a potential buyer, someone he knew and trusted. In that meeting he told us the price range they had talked about. Our initial assignment was to pull together definitive numbers such as historic financials and normalized earnings and help Sam work out a fair deal. He did not need top dollar. He just didn't want to be taken advantage of.

Unfortunately, we never got to that stage. In the next few weeks, Sam was diagnosed with brain cancer. Within months, he was dead. Sam's wife was left with little knowledge of the business and no transition or contingency plan in place. The potential buyer, we later heard, offered her less than half the figure that he and Sam had been discussing.

Sam's story underscores the main point of this chapter: because you never know when the unexpected can hit, business owners should take the time today to plan for it before it's too late. Business owners should consider their loved ones and have a plan at the ready, even if the potential planned transition is fifteen, twenty, or more years away. Having a solid plan with a focus on the end game and life goals is preferable to waiting until a crisis forces the issue. It means dealing with emotional issues sooner rather than later. And so, we have put a particular emphasis on this point. It's a theme that runs throughout this book. We focus on it because, in our experience, business owners are most successful when they grapple with and resolve such emotional topics as succession, transition, contingency, and legacy early in the life of the business.

There are strategies business owners can use to make the planning process easier. The next few chapters will cover those strategies in greater detail. The alignment of personal life objectives with the demands of the business is crucial. This sounds easier than it often is, but the process of aligning the plans builds the business, so it works for the owners rather than them working for the business. This also helps make transitions—whenever and however they occur—smoother.

Furthermore, we'll discuss how business owners should develop a comfort level in identifying and dealing with the right-brain emotional issues that are part of owning any business. We spend the next few chapters discussing in detail these and other ways owners can build their businesses for greater profitability and value and eventually plan for an exit.

CHAPTER TWO

The Hobby Gets Out of Control

Understanding Your Role as an Owner

Even before he was thirty-five, Gordon had achieved something most business owners dream of: making products he was proud of and selling them at a booming rate. His business, Woodworks, based in Indiana, produced heirloom wood furniture—tables, chairs, cabinets, and shelves—and shipped them all over the country. After the company started up in 1995, revenues rose steadily, eventually topping at $17 million. That success afforded Gordon and his family—originally small farmers—a prosperity that they had never imagined.

And to think, it all happened without any long-term formal planning. Gordon did not think strategically about the goals of the business, how to keep it sustainable over the long haul, or how it all fit into his life plans. The business seemed to run fine without all that. Or did it?

The Hobby That Got Out of Control

Before Woodworks started, Gordon was a small farmer raising chickens and a few crops. The cash flow was modest, but enough to afford him, his wife, and their two sons a modest living. As he was a third-generation farmer, it gave him the satisfaction of keeping a farm running that had been worked by his father and grandfather.

Just as important, it gave him control over his life. He had quality time with his family. And he had the freedom to indulge a lifelong hobby. He made and stained tables and other wood products in a corner of his garage. He sold them to friends and other local businesses.

Fate turned Gordon's life—and business fortune—around when a furniture distributor visiting the area noticed one of the tables in a cafe. He ordered a few. Suddenly Gordon's handiwork attracted a wide following. Orders started flying in. Thirty from Detroit. A hundred from New York City. Eighty from Boston.

Gordon took on the challenge. He hired dozens of employees and opened new building spaces around the farm. His passion was no longer a hobby. He was a business owner who devoted all of his time and energy to making the business a success. It was a role he accepted even though he did not have the skills to manage a midsized company, as he would be the first to admit. And yet, he managed to carry on and ride the wave for about fifteen years.

At that stage, fate struck again, this time with trends that affected the business negatively. Consumers' tastes started to change, and without strategic planning, Gordon was unaware of the threats in the industry. Furniture retailers switched to ordering directly from China. Labor and benefit costs continued to rise. Gordon felt he was not in control. Things were happening around him, and he did not have a plan to combat them. Within three years, the company began to lose tens of thousands of dollars per month. Revenues fell 60 percent.

Gordon did all he could to save the company. He mortgaged everything he had to keep it going. Ultimately, the same kind of uncontrollable wave that brought Gordon prosperity was threatening to destroy everything he owned.

The business was in crisis mode. With nowhere else to turn, Gordon acknowledged that he needed professional guidance. Could we help?

Gordon's story—or some version of it—is one many business owners have experienced. Like him, most owners are hardwired to put the demands of the business first. Particularly in the early stages, they need to play an active, hands-on role in every aspect of the enterprise: new hires, management changes, setting production goals, maintaining quality control, customer satisfaction, resolving disputes, and so on.

For a lot of business owners, Gordon's roller coaster record of earnings also rings familiar. The arc of Woodwork's earnings and losses—an early upswing, followed by a dramatic downturn, and then a mad scramble by the owner to keep things afloat—is not uncommon, especially among new businesses. There are periods when the cash flow is strong followed by long stretches when the owner struggles to make payroll. As business advisors, we have worked with dozens of businesses that have gone through just that kind of cycle.

But what Gordon had most in common with many other business owners was not something he had, but something he lacked: a clear game plan. He had no strategy for the business or his personal life nor a blueprint for achieving either. From the time Woodworks started, Gordon was so busy keeping the supply of his products flowing to meet the heavy demand that he never took the time to make a plan.

The company's early success resulted in no small part from Gordon's ability to move quickly to build a company that could meet a huge, unexpected demand. He quickly hired a team of capable employees. And he personally made sure that Woodwork's products were consistently top quality. When demand declined, he was too preoccupied with trying to meet payroll, stave off creditors, and keep the company afloat to take the time to formulate a plan.

> *And yet, the difference between the owners who plan for their futures and those who operate based on chasing daily fires is clear and stark.*

As a business owner without a plan, Gordon was in good company. Of the hundreds of business owners we have worked with, only a small percentage have taken the time to create a game plan by the time they contact us. And when they do have plans, they rarely include the kind of comprehensive strategy that is needed.

And yet, the difference between the owners who plan for their futures and those who operate based on chasing daily fires is clear and stark. Business owners who properly plan find that their destination is set, their direction is known, and they end up having a better quality of life while running the business. They are also more likely to achieve a higher level of goals. And when the time comes, they will be better prepared for their exit, whether it is for unforeseen health issues or part of a strategically planned transition. Those without plans end their day wherever the tornado winds drop them, only to get caught up in the cyclone again the next day.

The consequences of not having a plan can be catastrophic. For some, it's a key reason for early failure. The statistics on the rates of closure for new businesses are daunting. Around 50 percent of businesses fail within the first five years, and 70 percent in the first ten, by the account of the Small Business Administration. In many of those instances, the business could likely have been salvaged if the owners had some sort of strategic plan.

Often the owners who manage to beat the odds and survive end up hitting a wall or muddling through with little growth. Only 4 percent reach revenues over a million dollars, and only .4 percent achieve revenues of over ten million, according to a 2008 Small Business Administration report.[1] Many owners who push through and survive become overworked from putting out daily fires and are unable to enjoy life or reap the advantages of ownership.

Researchers have documented the success of entrepreneurs and business owners who take the time to create game plans. A survey of graduates of Harvard's MBA program—reported to have taken place in 1979 and noted in several books and publications[2]—could be instructive. The graduates were asked: Have you set clear, written goals for your future with plans to accomplish them? Eighty-four percent answered that they had no plan. Thirteen percent had a plan but did not write it down. And only 3 percent had written goals and plans. When the same group was surveyed ten years later, the 3 percent with well-defined written plans were earning ten times the rate of the other 97 percent.

---

1   The Small Business Administration, "The Small Business Economy," 2008, sba.gov/
     sites/default/files/files/sb_econ2008.pdf.

2   Mark H. McCormack, What They Don't Teach You at Harvard Business School: Notes
     from a Street-Smart Executive (New York, Bantam: 1986).

The Business Life Cycle and Your Role as an Owner

Creating a strategy requires more than crunching numbers and plotting how to reach production and sales goals. It is a multistep process that usually calls for the business owner or owners to work closely with an experienced business advisor or an advisory board made of peers who can guide them through common landmines and look at the business unemotionally. Having fresh eyes look at something often brings immediate positive changes and results.

We can confirm that every business is unique, but the lifespan of businesses typically runs in phases—starting with incubation and proceeding, usually many years later, to full maturity. There are also various cycles in between as circumstances change. Business owners should be aware that demands of ownership—and the strategic thinking required to keep the business on a path of success—may differ with each cycle.

Ideally, the planning during the startup phase should be about articulating a clear vision about the reason for starting a business. Before signing a lease for a workspace, hiring employees, or seeking financing, aspiring business owners should ask themselves what their reason for starting the business is. The most common answer is that the business will provide the funding to support a lifestyle for themselves and their family. While that might make short-term sense, it embraces only a narrow part of what a business can and should be achieving. A more compelling set of objectives, in addition to providing for current lifestyle, would be to (1) meet a need that exists in the market for a new or better product, (2) to build business growth and value, (3) to protect and accumulate wealth, (4) to support the local community, and (5) to protect loved ones and provide them with opportunity and/

or security. A mindset centered on these goals will eventually help position business owners to pull themselves away from the day-to-day scramble of running a business and devote themselves to strategic planning.

Michael Gerber, the internationally renowned business guru, has brought a lot of clarity to the kind of mentality entrepreneurs should have to start and run successful businesses. Gerber argues that most new business owners are technicians with technical skills and don't enter business as strategic thinkers. The owner's role, he said in his book *The E-Myth Revisited*, should be to "create entrepreneurial strategies to grow a company, to grow the client base, to increase profit, to show an increase in return on your investment."[3]

The next phase of business usually kicks in once the business reaches a level of growth beyond the startup phase. This is certainly when business owners should begin establishing and aligning their business and personal end goals and objectives into their planning process if they haven't done so already. On the one hand, this requires calculating the financial end goals, however they define it. It could be a ten-year plan or a thirty-year plan. They can figure out the level of cash that will be needed from the business to maintain the standard of living that they want both before and after they exit the business. Too often the scramble to maximize profits leaves owners thinking that the planning should be all about the business and not about their personal ambitions. From our viewpoint, both must be considered together. With clarity about both, owners can then create a holistic plan that aligns their personal goals with business strategies. If there is a wealth gap—a difference between what the business can earn and what owners require to support their lifestyle and legacy objec-

---

3   Michael Gerber, The E-Myth Revisited: Why Most Small Businesses Don't Work and What to Do About It (New York, Harper Business: 1995).

tives leading up to and following a transition—there must be a plan for bridging the gap. And—just as important—there might be a life gap—a status when business owners have personal goals they have not fully accomplished. A sound plan must include ways to assure that owners are able to bridge the life gap as well. This will position owners to be both financially and emotionally prepared to exit the business.

Here, too, Gerber offers insight. "Once you recognize that the purpose of your life is not to serve your business, but that the primary purpose of your business is to serve your life," he wrote in the *E-Myth Revisited*, "you can then go to work on your business rather than in it, with a full understanding of why it is absolutely necessary for you to do so."[4]

Even at this stage of the business cycle, owners who are also hoping to incorporate their eventual exit from the business into their planning should be clear about the emotional aspects of transitioning to the next phase of their life after business ownership. Whether the exit is in three years, five, ten or twenty, to help ensure it's successful, time is needed for both its planning and execution. And the more time, the better. The planning will include setting an initial transition target date. Depending on the age of the owner, this may be nothing more than an educated guess, which would need to be fine-tuned over time. The important thing here is that there is an initial target to plan for. The planning will also require giving thought to the lifestyle the owner envisions after transition and what kind of legacy he or she wants to leave. Again, depending on the age of the owner, these too will be fine-tuned as the owner matures. This emotional aspect of planning, as we discussed in chapter 1, is often the toughest part for business owners to engage in. Many owners avoid it because they don't want to deal with the emotional aspects of transitioning out

---

4   Gerber, E-Myth Revisited.

of the business or putting the business up for sale. Often, they have devoted so much of themselves to the business that they can't think of doing anything else besides running the business.

As the business becomes more mature, owners enter a period where it's important to be clear about the value drivers that pertain to their particular businesses and their lives.

Pinpointing those drivers would mean addressing such questions as how much the business relies on the owner or key personnel or how much earnings fluctuate. Gaining clarity about the drivers will help inform owners about the kinds of steps needed to make a business more profitable, more valuable, and more sustainable, especially when the time comes to sell or transition the business. The fewer risks a business has, the more appealing it will be to a potential buyer. The guidance of an outside professional advisor can be crucial in identifying and monitoring the relevant value drivers.

During each phase of their business's life cycle, owners should write down their plans.

During each phase of their business's life cycle, owners should write down their plans. Putting the strategy on paper gives owners a blueprint that they can refer to as they move forward. Having everything in writing also makes it easier to make adaptations if and when they become necessary. A tight plan outlined over a few pages with bullet points works best for most business owners rather than an overworked tome. The Harvard survey mentioned previously shows that entrepreneurs who write down their plans are more successful than those who simply have plans but do not put them in writing. "Reduce your plan to writing," advised Napoleon Hill, an early expert on entrepreneurship. "The moment you complete this, you will have definitely given concrete form to the intangible desire."[5]

Each of the steps we outline is important in the creation of a viable game plan. Addressing them demands focus and time. Some of them also require research—into everything from the financial status of the owner to market conditions and other aspects of the business. Working with an advisor who has expertise in planning, building growth, and transitioning can be crucial in coming up with—and executing—a sound plan. In our experience, the earlier owners start this process, the better. Starting early will allow owners to come up with a strategy that maximizes value and allows them to reach personal goals. Even if planning is not done at the outset because of the head-down survival mentality when starting a business, owners should still undertake it at the earliest stage possible.

The Hobby Becomes a Business

When we started working with Gordon, we quickly learned that he had taken very few of the steps that we recommend business owners work through to create a plan.

What was most glaring was the lack of coordination between Gordon's personal and business goals. Gordon had a great passion for the business when he first started. But after several years, that passion started to fade. When making furniture was simply a hobby, he was happy, and his time in the garage was precious and creative. Now, making furniture—compounded by multiple orders and new design requirements—was stressful.

He had also sacrificed the one thing he prized most—control. He had done his best to lead Woodworks through the early phase of

---

5   Napoleon Hill, *Think and Grow Rich* (Meriden, CT: The Ralston Society: 1937).

strong growth. And he had devoted considerable energy and resources to keeping the company afloat when it began to encounter challenges. Gordon lost control of his own destiny and was forced to react to things around him as they came. At times he made great decisions. But he also made his share of ill-advised decisions. He did not possess a master plan. He was resigned to doing everything he could to ride the wave underneath him and hold on. And on top of that, as owner, Gordon had almost one hundred employees to manage. Success had come at a pretty heavy price. It brought him anxiety and misery.

In our early conversations, Gordon made clear what he wanted most: to stop the business from losing money and return it to a profitable status. He wanted to maintain a leadership role but one that would allow him the time and space to pursue his first passion—working directly with furniture. He also wanted to involve his wife and other family members in the management of the business. And perhaps most important, he wanted to regain control of his own life. For Gordon, that mostly meant having more time to himself.

From our point of view, this was a turnaround situation. We could not rely on how things were done previously. We had to create a provisional plan, and we had to get Gordon to believe his business could and should be run differently.

In consultation with Gordon, we established three main objectives. The first was to stop the hemorrhaging. The second was to develop a strategic plan toward business sustainability. In other words, we had to create a blueprint to keep the business running for the long term.

And third, we were tasked with helping Gordon reclaim his personal life and passion. In fact, the goals fit the model of establishing business goals and personal goals together. As we mentioned as part of the discussion of the second phase of a business's life cycle, the two go hand in hand.

Once we had a firm sense of the objectives, we began a deep dive process to truly understand the current state of the business and the environment it operated in. This is an extensive procedure that should not be taken lightly or overlooked. In order to know how far you have to go to reach your goals, you first need to know exactly where you are and what you're starting with. We spent several days in and around the business, analyzed the industry and competition, solicited feedback from key employees, and finally engaged the team in a detailed business diagnostic of both the external and internal environment.

A business diagnostic can best be described as a business CT scan and is often referred to as a SWOT analysis. It attempts to look at every aspect of the business. In this case, it allowed us to identify Woodworks' strengths, weaknesses, opportunities, and threats. We brought the Woodworks team into the process, which also allowed us to identify any gaps in opinions between Gordon and his team. To move forward in a positive manner, the entire team needs to be in alignment. So the differences that surfaced became an integral part of our improvement action items.

While the framework of a SWOT analysis might be simple to understand, we urge business owners to use an experienced professional to facilitate it because the more extensive and transparent you can make this step, the better the results in the strategic planning process.

After the deep dive analysis, we helped Gordon take some important stopgap measures to regain the financial stability of the company. They included laying off some employees, dropping employee benefits, and developing a financial plan to get the business back to break- even.

To build more long-term security for the business, we also developed a plan to combat competition from China. The one thing China could not do is provide custom finishes on the furniture. China was just better at selling you a container full of the same product. We helped devise a marketing and operational plan to offer consumers the ability to order furniture from the retail floors and select one of several finishes (stains) based on their tastes. Customers could also order furniture on a two-tone basis.

Just as crucial as stabilizing the business was how we could help get Gordon back on track with his personal objectives. We elevated his role from strictly doing day-to-day management. His new status gave him time to make decisions as they relate to the game plan and labor reorganization to drive the business forward. It also allowed him the space to focus on what he liked best—working with wood.

Gordon took advantage of the systems we put in place and focused his attention on growing revenue by diversifying his customer base. He also started a search for an experienced professional to run the sales side of the business. After a few failed attempts to find the right person, he settled on his son-in-law, Dave. As sales manager, Dave quickly learned the business and was able to drive sales expansion throughout the country.

Within two years, Woodworks had returned to financial stability. As a result, in part due to increased sales nationwide, orders rose to $1.2 million a month. With that increase, there was now more demand for Woodwork's products than the company had the capacity to meet. Gordon's wife reached out to us again, requesting guidance on how to best handle the increased demand.

This marked a new phase in the company's life cycle. And with that cycle came a new set of challenges—a pretty common problem for a company. This time, we, Gordon, and some of the other managers were better prepared to work together to address the challenges. As a result of our earlier work together, the company had established a stronger foundation to address challenges.

After the analysis, our most important step was to redesign the flow of operations.

Originally all orders were tracked manually via paper copies. We implemented a basic system to track orders as they came in, manage production planning, identify customers' purchasing trends, and control the inventory supply chain.

We also recommended other steps. Some examples include buying new equipment to speed up processes; more accurately calculating proper batch sizes and thereby streamlining the operations; and communicating production needs more clearly so that employees know exactly what is expected of them each day. Further, we suggested the company rely more heavily on key managers to run the various departments. Some of them had been in place for years and just needed the opportunity to step up and assume more responsibilities. By tweaking the existing structure of operations, Woodworks was able to handle the increased demand. The changes gave the company the capacity to meet a higher demand of up to $2 million in orders a month if sales continued to climb.

Gordon's case illustrates the kinds of steps that can be done to save a business without a formal game plan or help make a productive company better or more productive. When we disengaged from the business, the company had returned to positive growth. It had a plan for possible further expansion and a management team that took on some of the day-to-day responsibilities. This left room for Gordon to do what owners should do: strategize for the future.

> *For a plan to work well it must be centered around both business and personal objectives.*

The story of Gordon and his business highlights the importance of creating—and executing—a game plan. But it also illustrates that for a plan to work well it must be centered around both business and personal objectives. And, finally, Gordon's experience shows that every business works in cycles—and they face different challenges in each cycle. Even the best of plans must be readjusted—sometimes dramatically—with every cycle. This requires owners to be strategic thinkers rather than technicians.

Taking on the role of a strategist is much easier and more logical if owners organize their business so that they are running it rather than the business running them. We devote the next chapter to a discussion of why this is far more than a catch phrase and how you as a business owner can make it happen.

CHAPTER THREE

Taking Control

Making the Business Work for You

I n the last chapter we detailed the story of Gordon, a business owner who ran a successful business but lacked a game plan and suffered the consequences. We decided to devote this chapter to explaining how every business owner can avoid that fate and begin the path toward the graduate level of business ownership. From our experience, once owners have established a stable level of productivity and profitability in the business, they should step back and take stock of where they are and how best to move forward. It's an important process, one that no owner should overlook or diminish. For those who are seeking to advance from the frantic state of continuously working in the business to a state of working on the business, it's essential.

This process of taking stock is threefold. The first step calls for owners—and their spouses or significant others—to have discussions on each of their individual personal goals and the things that bring them their greatest excitement and fulfillment—in essence a discovery of their value drivers. From our perspective and experience, this is best accomplished with outside assistance from experienced advisors who can offer guidelines on the approach and provide insight and pushback.

The goals often differ greatly according to the owners' age ranges, among other factors. It's not unusual for owners in their twenties or thirties to have objectives that are focused on the business—such as how to enhance value as quickly as possible. By the time they reach their fifties or sixties, owners tend to pivot their goals in more personal terms. They shift from an achievement mindset to one of quality of life and meaning. This difference in emphasis between owners of different generations also surfaces in the other steps of this process. Just as businesses experience different cycles, owners too, go through phases. And business owners' goals and needs often shift as they evolve from one phase to the next.

The second step is to conduct a financial needs analysis in order to quantify how much money or assets they will need to meet their objectives from step one. After establishing a clear sense of both their personal goals and financial needs, business owners will be in position to take on step three of the analysis. That involves determining exactly where they are via an honest and thorough review of the business and then calculating how much the business has to grow in profitability and in value and in what time frame, to successfully reach their financial and nonfinancial goals. As owners undertake this analysis, another important question inevitably arises: Is the business dependent on the owner or the other way around? The search for an answer to this question is an important part of the process of taking control of the business.

These assessments—and their overall objective of uncovering where owners are and where they are headed—is usually challenging, in terms of both time and emotions. That's one reason we feel that most owners are better off starting the process after they have hit significant forward momentum in the operation of their business. Sometimes startup survival requires the owners to put their heads down with all-out energy to make sure cash is coming in to cover payroll and provide necessary funds needed for the company's initial growth. Once business owners are out of that mode and feel they can lift their heads up to breathe a little, it would be a good time to look deeply at where they are and where the company is headed, including its financial potential. So let's dive deeper into these three steps.

In the Pursuit of Happiness

For many owners, pinpointing personal goals and objectives can be taxing. It requires them to be introspective and to consider some probing topics—such as what their core value drivers are. These are the kind of emotional topics that most owners avoid in favor of engaging in meeting day-to-day demands and financial benchmark goals. In our experience, however, addressing these issues is a critical success factor in ensuring that the company becomes the vehicle to help the business owner achieve their personal "end" goals and not be a vehicle that continuously demands the owner's time, resulting in the owner losing control and requiring him or her to serve the business.

In our practice, we start by having the business owner and their significant other independently answer a few questions about themselves and some of their goals. We often describe this as a "What's It All About, Alfie?" questionnaire. Here are examples of some questions we ask: What would be the best use of your time and talent? What makes you most excited to wake up in the morning to another day? What makes you happiest in your life? What do you want more of in your life? What makes you feel accomplished and good about yourself? What are you most proud of accomplishing in your life?

The value isn't so much in the answers to the questions. The real value comes from the robust conversation we have afterward, thus our recommendation of enlisting an experienced advisor to facilitate the process. Only after uncovering their core values—and identifying goals and those things that are most important to them—are owners in position to plan how they can achieve those goals. As a case in point—if they place a heavy premium on having time to themselves on a regular basis, the discussion might turn to ways to structure the management of the business to make that possible.

This will often be the first occasion many business owners work directly on identifying things that are important to them—on weighing their short-term goals and long-term goals and drawing a connection between them. As advisors we keep a detailed account of these conversations, including our assessment of the best course of action for owners to take to achieve their goals. Later, if they lose sight of or veer away from their value drivers, bringing them back to the conversations can serve as a reminder of what's really important to them and the thinking processes that went into identifying them.

Age, family circumstances, and other factors can play key roles in determining personal objectives. And sometimes those objectives are informed by uniquely personal wishes or circumstances. One question many business owners ponder is how much time and energy they want to give to work versus personal pursuits. Some business owners are comfortable spending eighty hours a week in the business and sacrificing much of the time they would give to their personal lives to the business. Others prefer limiting the time they give to the business and devoting more time to fulfilling their personal goals. For most business owners, the work/life balance equation changes at different cycles of their lives. What's important is for the owners to have clarity about how much time they want to work or spend on personal activities and meeting personal objectives at each stage.

How Much Will You Need to Achieve Your Objectives?

The financial needs analysis, step two in our process, is an integral part of establishing personal goals. It calls for owners to get an estimate of how much money they and their family require to finance their lifestyle and personal objectives outlined in step one—both currently and in the future. Here, too, the age of the owner can play a big role in the calculations. A younger generation of owners is more likely to focus more on their current needs. As they get older and particularly as they move closer to the time they might want to sell or transfer the business, owners often consider not only how to finance their current lifestyles but also how much they will need after they have transitioned to life after owning the business.

The financial needs analysis typically starts with a conversation between the business owner and a professional advisor. The opening questions can be basic—such as how much money the owner and their family spend after taxes and their financial objectives for the future. Business owners, however, should also be prepared to address a more detailed set of questions about the cost associated with the objectives they outlined in step one—during and after business ownership.

Business owners who haven't done advanced planning and are thinking about transitioning out of the business in the short term will have a deeper dive into cash needs than an owner that is many years away from their exit. Projecting the standard of living owners want to have after exiting a business is important. Some owners might envision spending a significant amount of time traveling. Or they might have in mind situations where the extended family, including children and grandchildren, spend more time together. The earlier business owners are able to pinpoint their goals, the more time they have to make them a reality.

The Millers, a couple who own a business in California, provide a great example of how a financial needs analysis can be useful for owners planning an exit. By any measure, the Millers' business was successful: The owners knew they wanted to transition out of ownership in ten years. They were also in sync about their primary personal objectives: to spend more time with family. That could involve anything from destination vacationing together to having a home to serve as a family retreat in which to spend quality time with their children and grand-children by the poolside. And they were also clear about the kind of lifestyle they wanted to lead after business ownership and how much it would cost.

Even though they were lucid about their personal goals, the couple still found they could benefit from some guidance. They had devoted so much of their resources to financing their children's education and other day-to-day expenses that they had not set aside investment savings to finance their retirement. The main focus of our work was devising a transition and exit plan to transfer management responsibilities and ownership to their son in conjunction with ensuring the long-term sustainability of the business via a business growth and increased profitability plan to fund their retirement savings. With their projected date of transitioning out of the business a decade away, there was time to come up with a solid plan to start acting on it. We devised a five-year plan, the processes needed to get there, and the necessary execution steps to drive the business to support that vision. On the personal side, this required some reorientation of their budgeting.

They deferred some of their current fun spending in order to accelerate the paying down of their personal and business real estate mortgages. Following that discipline as their personal number-one priority, when the transition came, they would have more resources to fund not only their postbusiness lifestyle basic needs, but also all of their planned family adventures. We are happy to report that the ten years just ended with both the business and personal plans executed very successfully and the business, son, and parents all thriving.

Can the Business Finance Your Dream Life?

As the case of the Millers illustrated, when everything is working, the business should be the catalyst for achieving a business owner's personal goals. Determining whether the business is performing well enough to meet those goals is where the thorough and honest review of the business comes in.

This review is the third step in our process. It includes validating the business model and determining the value gap or potential value gap, which, as we discussed earlier, is the difference between the business's estimated current enterprise value and the value required to support their current and future lifestyle, personal goals, and financial objectives.

We often see business owners who have revenue goals they want to reach as part of their accomplishment drive. But part of developing as a business owner is the conscious focus on business value and whether the owners are

> *When everything is working, the business should be the catalyst for achieving a business owner's personal goals.*

doing things to increase its value to close the value gap or whether their plans of action are diminishing the business's value and increasing the value gap by default.

When there is a value gap, there are different ways for owners to address it. For starters, it involves evaluating the current state of the business and the industry in which it operates, analyzing its strengths and weaknesses, and projecting various planning timelines needed to execute corrective action steps in order to close the gap. Here are examples of value drivers that historically drive business value up. Businesses that lack these drivers usually experience reduced value:

+ Above-average industry earnings and owner(s) compensation

+ Management team in place and operating the business

+ Systems and processes for every area of the business

+ Skilled people and great culture

+ Proven track record of documenting and executing a strategic plan for growth while building business value

+ Business's ability to run independently of the owner's daily involvement

Closing a value gap requires business owners to introduce a detailed vision and strategic plan.

Developing the right culture in the business is also key to assuring that the business stays on track fulfilling the plan. It is a rule of thumb in business that a good thriving culture is more important than strategy. Sometimes changes in the culture are required, and they can be the hardest thing to implement and keep in place. When a business owner identifies detractors, for example, they need to remove them. This is part of the commitment owners must make to assure that the plan is executed.

The Power of Clarity

For Adam, another owner we worked with, having a clear sense of his goals played a decisive role in his success starting a business, laboring to build its value, and eventually navigating an exit. The story of Adam—who was thirty-seven when the business launched—also shows how owners at a relatively young age can make their business work for them. Adam was a mechanical engineer in the midranks of a global Chicago-based quality control (QC) company when he pulled together all of the financial capital he had, pooled resources with a couple of colleagues, and launched a business. Six years later, he sold the company at a considerable profit. By forty-three, he was able to achieve the dream of financial independence.

In his engineer job, Adam had a good salary that afforded him a comfortable life and time for personal pursuits. But he had a vision of building a business of his own: an independent boutique QC lab. His knowledge of the QC market gave him confidence that there was a place in it for a small, personalized lab. He cashed in his 401(K) and all other savings and teamed up with two coworkers, James and Jay, to found OKLab. After a couple of years navigating the kinds of challenges startups frequently face, the business found its niche and started to achieve a measure of success. The three owners were the sole employees, and the lab was profitable enough to afford each of them a decent living.

But it did not take long for OKLab to start hitting hurdles. When the three owners began assessing their goals, it was clear that Adam and his business partners' objectives were strikingly different. James's and Jay's ambitions were modest. They were complacent with a business that gave them good salaries and a balanced life with ample personal time.

Adam's sights were set much higher. He envisioned transforming the business into a state-of-the-art QC lab. He was aware that the transformation would require significant investment in new equipment, a more modern design, up-to-date processes, and more of his time. The clear contrasts between the partners' visions inevitably led to conflicts and a decline in morale.

It was at this stage that the owners invited us in for advice on navigating a way forward. Since Adam owned 70 percent of the business, we started by guiding him through the three- pronged process of taking stock that we outlined above and engaged in similar discussions with James and Jay. The process validated Adam's ambitions for the business and positioned him to make—and act on—some key decisions. First, Adam bought out his partners. The process was fair to all sides, and with the status of sole owner, he was able to position himself to move forward, creating his dream business. This meant buying a building as a workspace instead of renting, bringing in additional personnel, introducing new systems, and developing a financial plan appropriate for a growing startup. It also required Adam to devote long hours to the business and sacrifice much of his personal time—something that he accepted as necessary to build value in the business. Recently divorced, he had more free time and was willing to give much of it to the business.

We met with Adam on a regular basis to review his objectives and whether they changed, discussed his financial needs analysis, and always looked at the business in case we needed to adjust or fine-tune any of the action steps to meet his objectives.

OKLab quickly gained a solid reputation in the industry. And, sooner than was planned, a larger, full-service QC lab began expressing interest in the company. Although selling quickly had not originally been Adam's plan, he warmed to the possibility. We worked with him to position the business for a sale. And, six years after starting OKLab, Adam sold it for nearly fifty times the amount he had cashed out of his 401(k). At forty-three, he was financially independent.

Two aspects of Adam's story were key to its success. First, as a business owner, he embraced the three-pronged analysis we recommend, along with the necessity for constant review. He started with articulating his goals and followed through with making the changes that were needed to achieve them. Second, when the moment was right, he had the flexibility to pivot from building up the business's value to selling it. He was able to make the business work for him.

Being Realistic and Transparent

No matter what their age, generation, or life situation, every business owner typically separates their personal objectives into primary, secondary, and other categories. As we mentioned earlier, a younger owner in their thirties will frequently have a primary goal of building a sustainable model for the business. That same owner's secondary goal could be spending time with his or her spouse and children. The planning process we outline here is intended to give owners the opportunity to sort out what priority they give to each of their goals—along with their level of commitment to each one. Goals that owners initially list might turn out to be nothing more than hopes, dreams, or "wouldn't it be nice" thoughts. True goals, however, should be something that someone really wants to commit to and work toward. Getting there can be hard work. Without commitment, it's not a goal at all but just wishful thinking.

Identifying goals—and indeed the entire procedure of getting the business to work for you—becomes even more complex for businesses which have multiple partners. The fate of the partnership that launched the QC lab we discussed above offers a glimpse into some of those complexities. Once the three business partners spelled out their objectives, it was clear that it would be impossible for Adam to make his vision for the business come true while working with his partners. If he was going to build a state-of-the-art QC lab, he had to buy them out.

The kind of differences the three founding owners of the lab experienced are not unusual. That's why it's imperative for each owner in a business partnership to go through the process of assessing where they are and where they and the business should go. From there, conflicting goals that would negatively impact the business's ongoing operations need to be laid bare in the open, fully discussed and planned accordingly. The planning process should coordinate and accommodate each owner's goals as best it can. But sometimes that's not possible, and the owners may need to take separate paths. Either way, it's important for the differences to be recognized and discussed with full transparency, to avoid owners just showing up to work doing their own thing, avoiding conflict, and hoping that things work out.

> *Even if business partners' backgrounds are similar and they have worked closely together, their lives and goals can diverge pretty dramatically.*

But not all business owners are as clear as Adam or as transparent about their goals. When partners do not take the time to clarify goals and plan for the consequences of fulfilling them, sooner or later, it will be apparent that things aren't really working out. Issues that may have been long buried come to the surface. And often those issues can negatively affect the running of the business. Even if business partners' backgrounds are similar and they have worked closely together, their lives and goals can diverge pretty dramatically.

This was the case with Craig and Terry, brothers who inherited TD United, a tool and die shop, when they were in their thirties. For more than two decades, they worked side by side as co-owners and managers of the business.

At first blush, the business partnership seemed to benefit both owners and fulfill their needs. It seemed to help that Craig and Terry had shared experiences and backgrounds. They were raised in the same household and had similar upbringings and education. Only six years apart, they also both belonged to the same generation.

But as the two and their business matured, some sharp differences emerged. One was in their family circumstances. Craig had two adult children who worked in the business, and he envisioned bigger management roles for them. Terry's children were still in school and not of working age. It was too early to determine what their future roles in the business might be.

Another disparity was in the amount of time the two owners wanted to give to the business versus their own personal pursuits. When he reached his early sixties, Craig, the older brother, decided to cut back on his days working in the business. Instead, he devoted a couple of days a week to camping and pursuing other recreational activities—pastimes that he did not have time for while working full time. Terry wanted to maintain a full-time schedule and continue 100 percent engagement with the business for the foreseeable future.

Even when the divergent approaches to the business surfaced, Craig and Terry avoided articulating their objectives and plans, let alone working through how the objectives and the process of fulfilling them would affect the business. Instead, they simply pursued their goals separately, perhaps hoping that things would work out. That created tensions between the two. Those tensions, in turn, negatively impacted the management of the business.

Craig and Terry's dilemma spotlights why it is important for all owners in a business partnership to be forthcoming about their personal objectives and to map out plans for realizing them.

Business partners should not assume that close friendships or family ties between them mean that they share the same objectives. Unfortunately in the case of Terry and Craig, they decided to continue to avoid dealing with their different objectives and desires in the hopes that these issues would fix themselves.

The effort it takes for owners to make the kind of analysis we have outlined here is considerable. But if done right, each individual step is very manageable. More importantly, it is an essential exercise in taking control of a business. When owners have achieved that control, the benefits it reaps for them and for the business can be substantial. There is no better illustration of just how beneficial making the right moves can be than the story of Daniel, owner of a successful technology company. He started the company, led it as a visionary, and achieved success beyond what he had ever thought was possible. By the time Daniel was fifty-seven and the company had been in operation for fifteen years, he received a multimillion dollar offer for the business, and to the surprise of many people, Daniel rejected it. Daniel conducted the kind of analysis we discuss here and was in the process of making some important changes in the management of the business. In other words, Daniel had a plan in place and wanted a chance to execute it. Seven years later, after receiving and rejecting multiple offers, Daniel sold the company for five times the initial offer

In chapter 5, we provide details of Daniel's story—how he built his company and then exited from it. But before that, we must address the crucial issue of the level of dependency of the owner on the business and vice versa. As you'll see, the business's dependency on the owner and alternately the owner's dependency on the business, often decreases its value. Lacking any other life pursuits, it becomes harder for him/her to ever leave. And when the owner does leave, their financial cash out is rarely enough to provide the happiness and personal fulfillment everyone searches for.

CHAPTER FOUR

Freeing Yourself

Do You Own Your Business, or Does Your Business Own You?

E ven the most adept business owners have considerable dependency on the business and vice versa. Much of that dependency is emotional, and it encourages many owners to feel that they need to spend more and more hours in the day-to-day operations of the business. We have devoted this chapter to pointing out ways business owners can reduce those dependencies. With that decreased role, business owners should have time and space to pursue other interests—such as hobbies, increased family time, physical activities, or other business interests. They will, of course, remain engaged in the business. In fact, they will actually have more unburdened time for strategic big-picture thinking as a result.

Getting to this stage requires commitment and time. To many business owners—who try to improvise—the process of decreasing dependence may seem daunting. In our experience, owners are most successful at decreasing dependency when they set it as a goal and follow through, step by step. To be sure, every owner and business is different. And so the procedures we prescribe can be adjusted to suit owners' peculiar situations. No matter how they get there, the prize for owners—where they have a balanced approach to personal time and to the business—is the holy grail. It should give them the confidence that everything—or most everything—in the business can run well without their direct engagement, in the hands of managers, for extended periods of time. We call this the graduate level of business ownership. It's the stage that most business owners often hope for and something all owners should strive for.

Still, for most owners, this stage remains not much more than an elusive dream. More often they are so keyed in on the day-to-day duties the business requires of them that time for strategic thinking, volunteer projects, family vacations, or any other personal activities seems too hard to work into their schedules. In fact, organizing the business to be less dependent on the owner—and the owner less dependent on the business—are goals that are not only possible to obtain but essential to having success both while operating the business and, eventually, upon exit. Below we discuss why it serves business owners to strive toward reaching those twin goals and how they can make that happen.

Why Reach for a Graduate Level of Ownership?

There are multiple benefits of decreasing mutual dependency by having an effective team in place that takes care of the business's day-to-day activities with limited owner participation. Achieving work/life balance is key. As we've emphasized before, getting that balance right can provide

> *Achieving work/life balance is key.*

a more fulfilling life, one in which business owners are able to thrive in the present while fulfilling personal pursuits, versus continuously putting things off to sometime in the future. Owning and running a business doesn't really have to be all in or nothing. Decreasing the mutual dependency between the owner and the business may even open up the option for the owner to maintain ownership while others take control of the management instead of someday looking to sell it—an option that is also appealing to many business owners. Whatever path owners take, owning a business should be about enjoying the journey along the way and not looking back years later, living in regret, and wishing time had been reserved to pursue other interests or accomplish other things. We don't believe anything else is as important as this.

The contingency factor—or the "What happens if?"—is another reason for working on the goal of decreasing the business's dependency on the owner. If a business is totally dependent on the owner for day-to-day operations, imagine what would happen to the employees, the owner's family—and indeed the whole business—if he or she suffers a major disability or premature death. Having someone who can step in to oversee and run things during a transition period can prevent a catastrophic ending.

Bottom line: when a company is dependent on a founder, and there is no succession plan in place, families, employees, and entire communities can suffer the consequences.

Also, business owners who pull back from work even just a little and pursue other interests are always far better prepared emotionally and psychologically for a successful life after business ownership. We discussed in chapter 1 how adjusting to a new life after the sale or transfer of a business is often devastating for owners. After years—and sometimes decades—of building their identities around a business, owners need to take the time leading up to the transition to redefine themselves and their missions. They may even enter a danger zone if they have put little or no thought into what they'll do directly after the sale and plan for the next phase of their lives, or, as one of our clients put it, how to deal with the void that is abruptly created, after "the phone [at work] stops ringing." The business that owners have poured so much of their lives into is a huge, dominating part of their identity. To give it up means risking a plunge into an existential crisis.

Besides making good sense for operating the business more efficiently, addressing contingency risks, and the opportunity to live a more fulfilling life and be better prepared for life after the business, a business that operates with minimal direct owner engagement is actually worth more. Simply put, such a business has stronger appeal to potential new owners than one that has heavier owner involvement and as a result can demand a higher purchase price. In other words, the more an owner can demonstrate that the business can function well without his or her constant presence, the higher price it is likely to yield, because having dependency on the owner carries greater risk to the buyer. The higher the risk, the greater the return the buyer is looking for, which decreases the value he or she will pay.

For example, if a business had a one-million-dollar EBITDA (earnings before interest, taxes, depreciation, and amortization) and because of the extra risk a buyer felt the business carried, they might tender a sale offer of only four times the EBITDA, rather than five times. In that case, the seller would find himself leaving one million dollars of value on the table.

The Challenges of Pulling Back

The story of Hal, a business owner we worked with, offers some insight into what can happen. Hal owned a busy, successful car dealership. Like many owners, he was the go-to guy in his business and was also deeply involved with the community. When he felt it was time to sell, Hal opted not to do a lot of deep dive personal planning. But in the course of informal discussions that we had with him and his wife Edith, Hal disclosed that he didn't really want to be at home with her all the time, and likewise, Edith didn't want Hal always at home with her either. She had her own routine and social activities, and she didn't want them to be interrupted. As much as the couple wanted to be together, they both knew they also had their own social circles and routines, and they needed space to continue their separate pursuits and not be around each other 24/7. Hal and Edith were more insightful than most couples, who don't foresee this kind of conflict until they are at home together for long periods of time.

To keep himself active and engaged after the sale, Hal bought a much smaller dealership. But the purchase of the new dealership wasn't scheduled to close until three months after the sale of his existing dealership. In the interim period, Hal and Edith headed to their second home in Florida. They were there together twenty-four hours a day, seven days a week, for twelve weeks. Neither was prepared for that. Hal in particular was at a loss. His identity, his jazz, was no longer there. In just ninety days, he became clinically depressed.

Hal's story is not much different from many others who don't fully consider what they'll do to fill in their newfound time directly after their exit from their business—to have something fulfilling they are going toward versus leaving something behind. A 2013 study by the Institute of Economic Affairs found that retirement increases the risk of clinical depression by 40 percent.[6] There's no getting around it. Proper personal planning is critical when the time comes to ensure a transition is successful, regardless of the chosen transition path.

Even business owners who accept that engaging in new pursuits is crucial to minimizing their dependence on the business can have a tough time identifying which new interests are a good fit. No owner we have worked with illustrates this better than Barry. After attending one of our exit and transition seminars, Barry contacted us. In his midsixties, he owned and operated a successful fourth-generation family business. His goal was to transition most of his management roles and responsibilities to his son, who worked in the business as part of the management team. If that transition worked well, the plan was for him to transfer ownership in the near future.

We plotted out a timeline and execution plan that met Barry's personal objectives and worked with the company to develop a plan focused on transitioning his management responsibilities and helping ensure the company's long-term sustainability. As the exit out of ownership and a full-time role for Barry got closer, a critical component of the plan was having a trial run with some of his "life after business" options to help him make decisions on what he was going to do to fill his time posttransition in a way that felt productive and satisfying.

During our discussions, Barry described the various charities that had reached out, inviting him to sit on their boards. Barry already served on a few nonprofit boards and thought this would be an interesting way to keep his involvement in the community and fill his

---

6   Gabriel H. Sahlgren, "Work Longer, Live Healthier," Institute of Economic Affairs, discussion paper 46, May 2013, iea.org.uk/wp-content/uploads/2016/07/Work%20 Longer,%20Live_Healthier.pdf.

time. But he also had a burning urge to pursue a passion he had for employee personality testing.

He decided to give this passion a practice run before his exit from the business. He attended classes in employee personality assessment and became certified. Soon he was out on the street offering his services to business owners he knew. Months later, Barry reported that he had contracted with a few companies. But he was struggling to balance finding the work, doing the work, and then having to go back out and find more work, all on a continuous cycle. A common description of this cycle is "eating what you kill." He acknowledged that he was not enjoying the hustle. Barry was lucky that he had taken a trial run of this new pursuit before he exited the business. We later learned that he had taken up some of the board offers that had been extended to him, and he was much more content.

The kind of shift away from regular hands-on engagement that Barry went through and that we recommend for others may seem logical and appealing. It is nonetheless hard for many owners. The difficulty, we find, is usually rooted in the struggles owners have in letting go. They consider their presence and skills indispensable for the running of the business. They are convinced that business operations will not function well without their stir. "No one can do it as well as I can," is one feeling they commonly express. "It will be a lot quicker if I just do it myself," is another.

As just one person, an owner can only give 100 percent on their best days. They tend to work really hard, invest a lot of hours, and most are really skilled at performing their duties, and as a result they believe they are the only ones who can perform the tasks right. We simply ask them to consider accepting that tasks can be done by others at a lower proficiency level while still providing above-average results.

In order to get the importance of the delegation concept through to them, we typically use an 80 percent proficiency level as a yardstick. But any percentage can be used based on the owner's tolerance. We then walk them through the exercise of delegating some of their responsibilities to other people. The idea behind this concept is the realization that if someone else can perform a task at an 80 percent proficiency level, the owner simply has to finish the remaining 20 percent or review the outcome. He or she is now able to free up significant time that can be dedicated to performing the more important tasks required by the business, dedicating time to strategic thinking, or taking time off to be with family or pursue personal interests.

Strategies for Decreasing Dependence

Whether it's problems with letting go or something else that keeps owners from working toward business independence, they would do well to conduct an honest review of how essential their level of engagement with the business really is. One way to make that determination is for them to ask themselves if they decided to take one or two months off from the business, could the business survive without them? If the answer is yes, congratulations are in order, as they've already achieved a status of independence from the business and are in much better shape than most businesses we consult with. But in most instances the answer is no. If that's the case, owners need to consider implementing a plan to lessen the business's dependency on them, or they will forever be trapped in the business and/or won't have

> *Owners need to consider implementing a plan to lessen the business's dependency on them.*

anything of too much value to walk away with, when they are ready to exit the business.

In our many years of advising owners on how to strategically grow their business's value and profitability, we have developed a set of tools to help them transition some of their management roles and responsibilities with the objective of decreasing the business's dependence on them and the other way around. We discuss each of the tools below. But a word of caution: rather than picking or choosing the one or two tools that seem most relevant or easiest to enforce, we strongly recommend that business owners embrace them together as an integrated package that is part of an overall strategic plan to increase the likelihood of their success.

DOCUMENT BUSINESS OWNER'S ROLES AND RESPONSIBILITIES

Owners should draft a list of all the tasks they perform for the business, the ones that only they do, and why. This exercise should offer a good picture of the current state of affairs. It will also identify responsibilities that can be delegated over time and establish priority of what can be more easily delegated first, in order to start reducing the business's dependency. In case anything happens to the owner, this record can also serve as a reference guide to ensure that the important duties are performed in his or her absence. Owners who can't find the time to catalogue everything they do in the business, can bring in an experienced outside advisor to conduct an interview to document everything from the most critical down to the not necessary. Once this documentation is completed, the more critical tasks needed to successfully operate the business should also be separately recorded and shared with key outside advisors, the management team, and in some cases with the owner's family.

BUILD AND DEVELOP A MANAGEMENT TEAM

Aside from being good business practice, hiring, training, and developing a strong management team is essential to decreasing the business's dependency on the owner. Owners should make it a priority to encourage managers to continually take on more responsibilities, to empower them to make decisions (and yes, to make mistakes as they learn), to identify and develop good middle managers, and to teach them how to build high-performing teams.

DELEGATE RESPONSIBILITIES

No matter what size the management team is—one person, five people or more—once managers are in place, the owner should start sharing management responsibilities and assigning some of the tasks listed in step one, in the prioritized order they were identified. Training to perform these duties should start with the administrative tasks that are the biggest drain on the owner's time. Each task should also come with an estimated learning timeline to ensure expectations are aligned and to properly balance how much is transferred over. The key to successful delegation is follow-up accountability to ensure things get done properly and timely. If not, corrective actions need to be taken.

GOOD RECORDKEEPING/TRUSTED INSIDER

It should go without saying that accurate, reliable record keeping is a must in running a successful company. On top of that, for an owner to start disengaging confidently, having a trustworthy manager overseeing finances or bookkeeping is critical. If owners are away from the business, they can't be worried about what is going on with the finances back at the shop. They need a responsible watchman or woman, someone handling the books who will look out for their best interests. Having that competent internal accountant or bookkeeper will be worth its weight in gold. It will give owners the confidence and peace of mind they need to step away and take some time for themselves.

INITIATE STRATEGIC PLANNING PROCESSES

It will be tough to run a business successfully for long without a clear direction and plan. We believe it is critical for businesses to have a *strategic vision plan*. That is why we highly recommend that business owners initiate strategic processes with their key personnel to ultimately develop the business direction or vision and the strategies to get them there, milestones to reach, and a financial projection to monitor progress. Again, accountability is critical for successful execution.

MANAGEMENT REPORTING SYSTEMS

Another crucial part of good management and delegation is ongoing reporting from the management team, including the accounting department. Owners should develop Key Performance Indicators (KPIs), both leading and lagging, which will allow continuous monitoring on how the management team is performing on the action steps needed to execute the strategic vision. It's important for both the owner and management team to stay informed about what is going on with the business and take any corrective action that is needed.

STRATEGIC BONUS INCENTIVE PLANS

To help ensure that the management team concentrates and executes on the strategic action items identified to meet the current year's goals (which is tied into the company's three- to five-year strategic vision), a bonus incentive plan should be put in place to reward team members for their dedicated efforts. Each manager usually has different tasks and goals, and thus each plan should be individually designed accordingly. With proper measurement as referenced above, the managers will know how they are doing on a regular basis. That usually leads to greater profitability and higher compensation for the individual. And it gives team members the incentive to continue minding the store when the owner is not around.

TAKE A VACATION

One way to find out how the business operates without the owner is for him or her to take vacations. Over the last twenty years, we have witnessed several businesses that seemed to actually operate better when the owner was away on vacation. Regardless, taking a vacation or time off from the business will not only train the team to work without the owner's direct supervision, but also allow the owner the time to relax and reenergize and possibly think about the next phase for the business—working on the business instead of working in it.

Two points about this package of tools are particularly important for business owners to underline. First, they can't be accomplished overnight either all together or individually.

Addressing them takes a process, one that starts with the business owner accepting that at some stage their 24/7 engagement in the business is neither necessary nor helpful to the business's growth and long-term viability. Owners can then tailor the tools to their own businesses and then commit to the time and procedures needed to fulfill them. Completing the whole process—from the personal plotting out of objectives to the strategic vision planning to the final, successful execution—takes a considerable amount of time.

Second, for the tools to work, perseverance on the part of the business owner is mandatory. An experienced advisor can be helpful in coaching and guiding business owners on starting and sticking through the process. But it's up to the owner to sign onto it and do the necessary follow through work.

> *An experienced advisor can be helpful in coaching and guiding business owners on starting and sticking through the process.*

The Importance of Persevering

Figuring out the right timing for owners to launch this planning is important. On the one hand, the older an owner gets and the longer he or she waits to start this process, the more difficult it is to complete. On the other hand, the very early period of ownership is not usually the best time either. The startup phase is often when owners commit their all-out attention and resources to the business. It's when they make a conscious decision to sacrifice their personal time and energy to whatever the business needs. It's not unusual for new or relatively new owners to spend sixteen-hour days at the office, go to bed thinking about management issues, wake up plotting how to close the deal with a potential major customer, and take calls just as a family dinner was starting that requires them to head back to work.

Adam, the technician we profiled in chapter 3, exemplified this startup mentality well. He left his job with a major quality control company and teamed with a couple of colleagues to start a boutique QC lab. After buying out his partners, Adam focused on creating a business that did not rely totally on him (even though it was hard work and required a lot from him). He gave all he had to the business. And the eventual payoff—sale of the business at a great profit—was worth it on both a financial and nonfinancial level. It provided him more time with his son and gave him the freedom of being able to do something, when he wanted to do it, without any negative financial consequences at a very early age.

Unfortunately, many owners lack the kind of insight Adam had, to know when to evolve beyond an all-out commitment to the business. Even after they have successfully led their company into a cycle of growth and higher earnings, many owners continue to surrender personal pursuits to the demands of business.

The experience of Mary, another business owner we advised, provides an excellent illustration of just how hard it can be for some owners to relinquish hands-on day to day engagement in the business, the kinds of problems that result from that need to maintain control and the importance of perseverance. After leaving a job with a large multinational corporation, Mary started a consulting practice that eventually grew into a good-sized business with several professional employees. The practice offered a marketable software that included dozens of large companies among its subscribers. Mary loved everything about the new company, from the day-to-day operations to the respect she received from others in the industry. Perhaps because of this, Mary unintentionally structured the business so that its success depended on her involvement.

Eventually, when the prospect of monetizing the company seemed real, Mary explored potential outside buyers. But she preferred the idea of transitioning the company—and, over time, selling it, to Elizabeth, one of her key managers.

Elizabeth was thirty years younger than Mary but nonetheless very capable. She acknowledged there were things she needed to still learn—financials, insurance, licenses, and other aspects of the administrative side—as preparation for eventually taking over. Motivated by the idea of one day owning the business, she was willing to learn.

Still, the transition was difficult regardless of their initial motivation and desire to proceed with it. Mary wanted to maintain control and oversight and did not relinquish responsibilities easily while Elizabeth, on the other hand, expected to be trusted more with the decisions she was making. Mary insisted that her oversight was warranted. Mary's reluctance to let go suggested that, in some ways, the business had come to own her rather than her owning the business, and the dependency was mutual.

Mary eventually agreed to sell Elizabeth 49 percent of the shares instead of the original plan of selling the business outright. As a result, the success of the business still depended on Mary's leadership, particularly as it related to the software.

Consequently, the struggle between Mary and Elizabeth continued. While they both had good intentions of making it work, inevitably there were tensions. Each of them made mistakes along the way—particularly in the way they communicated with each other. The transition and communication issues affected others in the company. Employees would sometimes go from one "parent" to the next in order to seek the answers to issues that arose that were more aligned to their thinking. On several occasions, we felt the need to act as mediators between Mary and Elizabeth. In particular, we needed to provide an objective perspective on several important decisions they had to make for the business.

Challenges notwithstanding, the two persevered. Three years after they became partners, Mary sold her remaining shares to Elizabeth and retired. Not surprisingly, since assuming the helm, Elizabeth has done an exemplary job as owner of the business. She made some of the decisions she wanted to implement while Mary was still around but could not. She has simply made the business her own.

As business owners begin to focus on decreasing dependency and, eventually, on transition, they can heed the lessons from Mary's experience and those of other owners we've profiled. For one thing, if a business has good foundations (in such areas as product services, customers, and systems) it can be transferred, and it does not and should not rely only on one person for continued success.

And also, remember that managers on the receiving end of the delegation are often much different from the owner and perform tasks in other ways. And that is all right. Businesses need managers and employees with different skills and approaches to make it work. The owner's way might not always be the right way.

But the point these experiences drive home best is how important it is for business owners to recognize when it's prudent for them to shift away from full throttle engagement in the business. There is no one-size-fits-all way of doing this. Transitions are personal to each owner. Mary, Barry, Adam, and the other owners all faced different challenges and followed different paths to get there, but they all followed the same underlying process we have outlined.

Each of these experiences also shows that the timing for owners to pull back is important. It's imprudent to wait until the last minute or the last year to implement the tools we outlined above. Owners also have to keep in mind that pulling back is part of a process. Before getting there, they must devote time and energy to coordinate their personal and business goals, as we outlined in chapter 3. They can then work on reducing their dependence on the business and the business's dependency on them.

If decreasing the dependency did not occur earlier in the business life cycle—which we highly recommend—we advise owners to at least begin this process three to five years before the planned business exit date for an owner to successfully prepare the business, to increase its value, and to remove the risk that the only way to fund the retirement is to sell at a reduced value or liquidate the business.

Decreasing dependency on a business does not occur overnight. It's a process that requires buy-in on the part of the owner and diligent follow-through. The examples we use throughout the chapter illustrate that process. Decreasing dependency is a crucial phase of business ownership, one that is essential to fulfilment of the owner's life goals.

CHAPTER FIVE

Running Your Business Like an Investor

Reaching the Graduate Level of Business Ownership

O ne question you might be asking yourself by now is: "Given all the challenges we described, what does it take for a business owner to transform a startup into a rock-star enterprise and pull it all together?"

For the best answer, you need look no further than the case of TechnoWorks, a software company launched in the mid-1990s that started humbly but with a sturdy foundation. Daniel and Edward, initially co-owners, were take-charge types and very committed. In their midforties, they also brought business know-how to the venture. In its first couple of years, the company's stature was modest: a handful of clients, a dozen employees, and roughly $1.5 million in sales.

Two and a half decades later, however, TechnoWorks' estimated value ballooned to above $60 million. The staff was more than one hundred. Multiple buyers began swooping in with offers. Daniel, now the sole owner, settled on a buyer and began to forge a deal. After intense negotiations he signed off on the sale of the company for more than he ever imagined when he first launched the business.

The remarkable deal was the climax of a dream-come-true story of business ownership and transition. However, the way Daniel adeptly managed and guided his business forward for twenty-five years is the real success story, the kind of narrative that every owner strives to have or at least learn from. Whether Daniel ultimately sold the business or even the amount he sold it for was not what defined this story as a success. Rather, it was the way he built the business and confronted challenges. Ultimately, he reached the enviable position of being able to sell the business when he really didn't need to. That's the status we earlier referred to as the graduate level of business ownership, something all business owners should strive for.

How did that happen for TechnoWorks? What enabled the business to go through that kind of growth and make such a comfortable landing? In fact, the business's story—the course Daniel took from conception through build-up and maturity—is instructive. In the previous chapter, we outlined the steps business owners should take to reach this level of business ownership. In this chapter we wanted to describe what occurred when an owner followed those steps—and went even further—to run his business as an investor would.

We worked closely as advisors to Daniel for most of the life of the business—a span of more than two decades. Over the years, the role we played shifted considerably, according to Daniel's and the business's demands and requirements. Among other tasks, it included coaching on how to grow the business to counseling on personnel and management challenges and objectives and, finally, helping position the business for the final sale. We found the path TechnoWorks took informative and enlightening. And so we are devoting this chapter to describing the details of it. Even if TechnoWorks might appear at first to be too big to serve as a model for smaller businesses, the path of growth it took offers lessons for almost any business owner. After all, business basics are fundamental for businesses of all sizes.

A Charismatic Visionary

Like many businesses, any story about TechnoWorks inevitably centers around its owner, Daniel. The business was his brainchild. He managed it in various ways, always with his own brand of creative and demanding leadership. Early on, Daniel conceptualized a growth path for the company and continuously made tweaks to it—some major, some small—to keep it on a fast track. He was engaged in both the minutiae and the big-picture strategic planning of the business. He applied his vision and creative thinking to developing and updating the various kinds of software TechnoWorks marketed, managing the staff and everything in between. Like every business, the company encountered issues and challenges and when it did Daniel focused on ways to tackle them, too. In the end, his all-in way of engaging in the business would, particularly early on, turned out to be its most important asset.

Daniel's role in the business, like that of many owners, progressed in cycles. In the early years, he gave his all to defining, investing in, and building the foundation for TechnoWorks. True to the startup mindset, he willingly sacrificed most of his free time, energy and capital to the business while monitoring every aspect of the business. Once the company stabilized, Daniel threw himself into growing the company, confronting challenges, and running and building a robust management team. Things did not work perfectly in the beginning. Finding the right people for management positions was an exercise in trial and error, and introducing new initiatives or product development projects took longer than he may have anticipated, but he never gave up pushing and sometimes pulling the company toward his vision.

As Daniel was able to assemble a good management team around him, over the years he began the process of pulling back from some of the day-to-day engagement in every detail. Giving the managers more responsibilities was essential because there was no way he could do it all and successfully scale the business. This, by the way, is the course of the owner taking control of the business—rather than the business controlling them—that we laid out in the last chapter. From there, once the business was beginning to run independently of him, he continued to strive to be a better owner and learn new skills or thought processes he could use to lead his team. He also began educating himself on the business exit and selling process with our help and got ready to navigate an exit from the business on his terms when the time was right. The cycles Daniel went through over a twenty-five-year time period roughly paralleled the cycles of business ownership that we outlined in detail in chapter 2.

It is also important to note that in his approach to running the business, Daniel used a mix of innovative and traditional methods. Some of them came from his own unique playbook. But he also employed strategies we describe and recommend for business owners in the previous four chapters. Among those strategies: understand your current state, build a management team, develop a management reporting system, formulate a contingency plan, and, ultimately, pull back for extended periods from daily engagement while the senior management team runs the business.

Yet, even when Daniel used traditional business approaches and tools, he infused them with his own ideas and hard-driving style. It was a style influenced, in our opinion, by Daniel's background as an endurance athlete. In his early years, he trained rigorously in distance running, long jump and other track-and-field sports events. He competed regularly and passionately. And he brought that intense sports experience—and especially the sense of discipline and competitive spirit it instilled in him—to business ownership. It seemed to make him constantly aware of his competitors and conscientious of the need to stay at least three steps ahead of them. The endurance athlete's soul guided Daniel throughout his tenure as a business owner.

If Daniel was the athlete turned business owner, our relationship with him over the years was much like that of a coach. Aside from recommending ideas, whenever TechnoWorks faced hurdles—we would be available to keep Daniel jumping over them rather than crashing into them. When he felt isolated it was our job to bring an outside perspective or act as a sounding board. "It is sometimes lonely at the top," Daniel told us often over the years. "And having you there to talk to was often very helpful."

Decisive Early Moves

The startup period is one in which business owners often throw themselves into defining their business and building its foundation. Daniel engaged in this phase like a hungry athlete, wasting hardly a minute in making bold moves. The first—and perhaps most important—was the decision about where to focus the business. The main products would be software with considerable potential to gain a broad range of clients. He chose products that were in an early stage of development and market acceptance. And for good reason: they would have space to be refined and updated. At the same time, the company's products had potential to acquire a wide clientele. So his vision was clearly defined.

Another decisive action Daniel initiated a few years into the startup phase was buying out Edward, his business partner. While some businesses work well with multiple partners as owners, being sole owner made sense in Daniel's case probably because his designs for the company were so focused. This status gave him the room to take the kind of full control of the business that he wanted and needed.

We recommend all businesses undergo a SWOT analysis at crucial stages in their development.

Following the buyout of Edward, it was also important for Daniel to assess the business's current state of affairs. We recommended that he conduct a SWOT analysis and he concurred. As you recall, this is a detailed look at a business's strengths and weaknesses in its internal operations and the threats and opportunities which define its external environment, all used in the development of the vision. By conducting the SWOT in the early stages of his own business, Daniel was able to identify the gaps between his vision and the company's ability to execute the strategies toward that objective.

Using data from the SWOT analysis and his own observations, Daniel was able to conclude that TechnoWorks, with all of its strengths and opportunities in the marketplace, had to devote enough attention to building the leadership team and systems, to address all the operational gaps and weaknesses in order to scale the business in the future and meet his objectives. His will alone was not enough. It now required purpose, thought, systems, and more importantly other people to get it done. Getting the business squarely on a sky-is-the-limit trajectory would become the primary focus of his life.

You Can't Do It Alone

As we mentioned, Daniel clearly recognized that achieving his goal was too big for one man to accomplish on his own. He needed a strong team—managers and staff. As part of his effort to beef up the senior staff, he engaged the whole team in a discussion about management flaws. This style of gathering—in which the whole team would take some time to reflect on issues facing the company— would become a regular annual event for the company.

The SWOT analysis also shined a light on a significant short-coming in Daniel's leadership style. For all of his visionary acumen, his skills at managing others were lacking. He was a perfectionist and expected everyone in the business to perform tasks as well as he could.

Delegation of authority was also an issue. Daniel would give his subordinates directives, but much was lost in translation. Daniel believed that he was effectively empowering others in the business with the independence to make decisions. His managers, it seemed, felt that Daniel was not delegating them with the rights and directives to decide things on their own.

Daniel used the critique to examine, and ultimately improve, his style of managing his team.

The analysis was enlightening. As part of Daniel's effort to address the challenges he was having managing people and his goal of assembling and leading a strong management squad, he ordered a personality match for every one of the employees at TechnoWorks, including himself. This specific evaluation is an extensive question-naire designed to pinpoint a worker's skills, strengths, and weak-nesses and, most importantly, to determine what activities motivate them—what's their source of energy. As a result, the match also assesses the test takers' personalities and helps identify the kinds of job functions that best suit them. The personality match is based on the concept that every business profits from having a team of employees with a range of personality traits. It is designed to help managers understand, tap into, and encourage the motivations and potential of each employee.

> *Corrective strategies and our assistance as advisors are worth little unless owners are committed to making a personal investment of their time by taking action and following through with execution.*

For Daniel, it made sense that everyone who worked in the business—senior managers, accountants, and all—undergo the personality match. He could then use the results to determine how each personality type best fit in the operation and how to get each to perform to his or her best ability. Since a big part of the objective was to find ways to better improve Daniel's own skills at managing people, it was also important that he, too, take the test.

In chapter 3, in our discussion of the issues that business owners Terry and Craig faced, we emphasized the high priority that owners should give to identifying flaws in themselves and their businesses and prescribing solutions. Accordingly, we worked closely with Daniel, suggesting tools and concepts we felt could help him. But corrective strategies—or, for that matter, our assistance as advisors—are worth little, we also noted, unless owners are committed to making a personal investment of their time by taking action and following through with execution. Daniel understood that and provided the necessary follow-through.

For the business to be all it could be, Daniel acknowledged that as hard as it might be, he had to work harder to develop a stronger management team. He used the information gathered in the SWOT analysis and personality tests to fine tune his team. It was composed of five managers, including a business manager, a sales manager and lead managers for each of the business's major software products. This team would eventually handle day-to-day operations. This allowed Daniel to focus more on strategic planning—just the leadership role that specialists of entrepreneurship suggest a business owner should play.

One of the concepts we proposed to help with managing the managers was the practice of management by objectives. That is a strategic model that is designed to improve the performance of a business by clearly defining objectives—and how the success of obtaining those objectives is measured—that are agreed to by both management and employees. Daniel agreed and introduced it. He and the senior managers would determine what the primary goals were and how they should be achieved and measured. This is a key part of the strategic vision plan that we discussed in chapter 2, and it turned out to be extremely helpful in Daniel's goal of honing his management skills.

Saying No to Millions

Seven years into the company's second phase, TechnoWorks hit its stride. The company's customer base was strong and growing. The staff had increased to more than thirty employees. Revenues had also risen—to around $7 million annually. And Daniel was plotting to expand the company even more. With such a solid company profile, it's no wonder that TechnoWorks began to attract the attention of potential buyers. A competing company made an unexpected offer to buy the business for $18 million.

For a business that had started from scratch just a short time earlier, it was a tempting proposition. The deal would have given Daniel a nice gain and the opportunity to exit the business comfortably and enter a new phase of life. After careful thought, however, Daniel rejected the offer.

Daniel had several reasons for that decision. For one, he did not feel that the prospective buyer was the right fit. For another, TechnoWorks was still on a solid path of growth. But the one thing that stopped Daniel most from agreeing to the deal was a feeling that his journey was not yet completed. With his drive for accomplishment, success, and getting the win, he was still eager—and well positioned—to bring his long-term vision for the business into fruition. Ultimately, Daniel was in control of his own destiny, he had a clear plan, and he knew that with a little more time he could achieve his targeted goals. Saying no to millions may appear silly to some but, done under the right circumstances, is simply evidence of an educated power position of control and a result of having a plan.

We hope that his decision—and the thinking behind it—will resonate well with business owners. Most owners commit an enormous share of their resources, time, and energy to the business and sacrifice much of their personal life along the way. Daniel belonged to the small handful of owners who take that commitment further, to the point that their abilities to lead are exhausted and/or they determine that the people or financial resources needed for further scaling calls for a much larger player. When an owner is driven to such an extent, that drive to reach the goal weighs more heavily than every other factor.

With the decision to push forward, Daniel started the next phase of ownership. The focus now was on expansion and edging ahead of his competitors. It was at this stage that Daniel's relationship to the business began to mirror that of a smart investor as much as that of simply an owner. But there was a major outstanding issue to address.

Protecting the Asset

TechnoWorks now had a multimillion-dollar valuation, resulting from the proposed offer. In our debrief with Daniel after his decision to reject the offer, we advised him to give priority to contingency planning. One reason was that he needed to protect what had become his most valuable financial asset. Daniel was married. He and his wife had a combined five children.

Providing for his family's future was one of his key personal goals. And yet, apart from his life insurance policy, there were no provisions to secure the future of the business or his family in case something happened to him. In chapter 1, we discussed how the survivors and the business are left vulnerable on a number of levels when business owners fail to introduce contingency and exit plans. Besides protecting TechnoWorks' value for his family, it was equally important for Daniel to put a plan in place to ensure the sustainability of the business and to protect his employees in case something happened to him. With our guidance, Daniel introduced a contingency plan consisting of three different parts.

When owners start contingency planning, the first step we often recommend is that they write a spousal letter. That is essentially an informational memo to the owner's spouse outlining what is going on with the business, who the key employees are, and what the owner would like to happen in case he falls ill or dies.

Daniel, however, needed to take this further. We advised him to create a family advisory board composed of a couple of senior business managers, his wife, one of his children, an attorney, and a representative from our company. The board met twice a year. It was designed to introduce the advisors to the family, educate them about the ins and outs of the business over time in order to prepare them for the potential day they might own the shares and have to make decisions.

In case Daniel died suddenly or was incapacitated, he wanted the family to be able to hold onto the company for at least one year, rather than selling it in what would appear to be an act of desperation. The semiannual sessions were useful in helping the family learn about the business and get acquainted with the managers as well as discussing the details of contingency planning.

Daniel also created an estate plan. As a lot of business owners do in the early stages of running a business, Daniel had put off preparing an estate plan to some other time in the future. Working with his attorneys, he came up with a plan to protect his assets and set up his heirs' trusts in the best and most efficient way that met his objectives.

Secondly, Daniel understood that it was crucial to formulate a strategy to retain essential employees and executive managers. Such a scheme would have two key objectives. The first was to encourage the employees who would be hardest to replace to stay with the company for the long run by investing in them. The second was positioning TechnoWorks for eventual sale by making sure that essential employees would stay on and run key areas of the company posttransition.

Working together with Daniel's attorney, we put forward a phantom stock plan, in essence, a stock appreciation plan that would reward those top managers who stayed with the company through the ultimate sale and beyond. This incentive package would also be there for the employees in the case of their own death or disability. Daniel delayed launching the plan until he felt he had the right management team in place. It took three years, but when those pieces were in place, he introduced it.

Not long after the contingency initiatives were put in place, Daniel received devastating personal news: a diagnosis of a life-threatening illness. While he underwent medical treatment, the advisory board stayed the course, making sure that all systems were in place in case he did not pull through or was going to miss a considerable amount of time. True to form, Daniel threw himself fully into recovery mode. In the end, he recovered fully. Still, having a contingency plan in place was helpful for the peace of mind of Daniel's business and his family during the most challenging circumstances they had ever faced.

The process of selecting the perfect second person in charge is a major challenge for any business owner and one not to be underestimated.

This turn of events highlighted the need for Daniel to make the final step toward completing the contingency plan and to stage the business for a potential sale: finding a successor. The process of selecting the perfect second person in charge is a major challenge for any business owner and one not to be underestimated. It involves imagining an individual who could take the reins and run the company, someone who shares the passion and vision as the entrepreneur, someone that the owner can see filling his shoes one day.

Pinpointing someone with Daniel's vision and hard-driving spirit made the search doubly hard. But Daniel knew it was necessary, and he approached it with his usual drive. We were there to assist in the process. As could be expected, there were trials and errors. This usually led to disappointment when, for one reason or another, they did not work out. Daniel even went as far as naming one person president of the company only for them to part ways eighteen months later.

Finally, a strong candidate emerged. Ray was an expert in the industry, someone who might be considered as a first-round draft pick to a company like TechnoWorks. When he became available, the company's advisory board discussed his potential hire at length. On the one hand, Ray seemed to have just the background and experience the business was looking for. On the other, hiring him would require a huge investment of money.

In the end, it was up to Daniel to make the decision about bringing Ray onboard. And so they met, and Daniel extended an offer to Ray, and he accepted. Given the strong and very different personalities of the two men, it was not, at first, an easy fit. But Daniel knew that it would require some give and take to make this relationship work. In the years since he had introduced the chemistry match to the business, he had become good at reading people, knowing how to communicate with them, how to manage them, and, more importantly, how to motivate them. Daniel's ability to work with Ray in spite of their different personalities showed just how far he had evolved in understanding and managing people.

The Graduate Level of Business Ownership

At this stage, TechnoWorks was operating smoothly. Recent hires had brought the number of employees to more than one hundred. Sales were on the rise, too. A reliable senior management staff was in place and functioning well. Daniel began to feel more comfortable delegating more and more of the running of the business to his upper management team. He and his wife, owners of a second home in

Florida, had started to escape there more often. Daniel had become more at ease than ever, living off the bounty of his successes. He and his wife soon decided to spend more extended periods in their second home—from December to May every year. Daniel would of course remain connected with the business and regularly check in.

But for an owner who had always been keenly engaged with every detail of the business, stepping back from day-to-day operations marked a major turn in Daniel's dependency on the business and the business's dependency on him. He was now definitely operating at the graduate level of business ownership.

With the company's successful business profile, it received a new offer, this time for almost four times the initial bid six years earlier. Again, Daniel declined. He was still not ready to let go of the company. But this time his reasons were slightly different. Things were working; he had a good quality of life and a balanced approach to running the business; and he was financially secure outside of the business and could simply wait. In other words, the best time to sell the business is when you don't need to, and Daniel was living his dreams without needing to sell his business.

But the offer ultimately prompted Daniel to think deeply about TechnoWorks' future and his own projected role in the company. Daniel and the business had been functioning smoothly for some years and could, in all likelihood, continue to do so. After two years and a careful review of the stress level of the business and his own status, however, Daniel made a major decision. His two and a half decades of ownership of TechnoWorks had reached a pinnacle. He determined that he had completed his mission with the company. He was now ready for the next and final phase of business ownership: exiting the business.

The company that had tendered an offer two years earlier returned with the sweetened deal. The timing seemed better than it ever had been before. Daniel agreed. Now he was tasked with negotiating the fine print and completing his exit.

There was still an emotional hurdle for Daniel to face. Having built TechnoWorks from the ground up and managing it ably for a considerable part of his life, was he ready to give it up and move to the next phase of his life? Even after agreeing on the sale and negotiating the terms of it, his feelings seemed mixed. It is probably not unlike the knot in the stomach an endurance athlete feels as he competes in his final competition. It was the last day of his last race, and he was headed on the final straightaway of the track. This sport was in his bones, and he knew he would never engage in it again.

Even though Daniel was, in many ways, a unique personality and business owner, his decisions and his way of running TechnoWorks offer some useful lessons for the majority of business owners.

Above all, from the startup to the sale, Daniel had managed the business on his own terms. His proactive visionary approach, creating the business and then following through with a step-by-step plan for its expansion, was exemplary. Daniel's way of giving the business strategic direction was also instructive. Many owners get bogged down with putting out daily fires or the daily demands of the business. Daniel always kept one eye on the future of the business. There is also a lesson in the way Daniel addressed his shortcomings. Often owners ignore red flags or delay dealing with the thorny issues that surface. In contrast, Daniel understood that with time and considerable effort, he could learn the skills he needed to manage his employees better.

And he eventually shifted from total hands-on engagement to delegating authority to senior management. But perhaps the most useful lesson of Daniel's story was how he stuck with his driving goal to build the business even when faced with tempting offers to sell it. Daniel's way of constantly devoting all of his energy, ideas, resources, and everything else he had into the business is what gave him more the profile of a major investor in his business rather than that of a traditional owner.

The fact that Daniel had mixed feelings about exiting the business right up to the end also offers a lesson. It illustrates how even the most focused, nimble owners have intertwined their emotions with the businesses they have nurtured. We will discuss this topic—and what it means for owners finalizing the transition to exit—in detail in the next chapter.

CHAPTER SIX

Letting Go

Stepping Back Is Often an Emotional Journey

One of the key takeaways of Daniel's story is that owners, over time, should have a focused effort on shifting out of day-to-day involvement. Later in the story, his efforts to align the company to the right buyer and the right timing shows the importance of and benefit for owners to be fully engaged in the formal planning process from startup to exit, as it gives them the power to control the outcome of when, how much, and to whom?

And yet, despite the firm hold Daniel kept over his business's management and the sale process, he still struggled with emotional issues during the period of decreased engagement with the business. He was in good company as we briefly touched base on in chapter 4. As it turns out, emotions come into play for everyone who steps back from a full hands-on role in managing the business, exits from business ownership, and enters a new stage of life. Every owner we have helped with this process—including each of those profiled in this book—experienced passionate emotional feelings during the process. Whether the progression away from the business is a matter of months or years; whether it's a sale or other type of transfer; whether it's owners who step back from an ownership role, deal with multiple business partners, or any number of other factors, emotions will inevitably surface. And, at least for some time, the impact of those reactions will likely be intense.

> *Emotions come into play for everyone who steps back from a full hands-on role in managing the business.*

We're devoting this chapter to pinpointing and exploring the different types of emotions that owners can expect as they prepare for, go through, or complete a shift out of the business and move forward to accomplish other identified goals and pursue their bucket list experiences. We also offer some tips on how these feelings can be mitigated or, at least, managed. It's crucial for owners to have clarity about the various ways a decrease in the dependency on the business can affect them emotionally. The more transparent owners are about the challenges of the intense sentiments they will face, the better chance they have to prepare themselves for the emotional reactions they will experience in the journey. That clarity will also help them make a smoother evolution away from day-to-day management and eventually to an exit that is financially successful, achieves their other life objectives, and allows them to move forward into something that is inspiring, rewarding, and fulfilling.

Owners need to realize that the management shift to the graduate level of business ownership can extend over a long period, often a matter of many years. And the stressful aspects of the process can plague owners for protracted periods, too, particularly if they do not identify the potential landmines and have a plan for tackling them.

Executing a plan takes time and that is why we highly recommend that owners focus on decreasing the business dependency on them early on in the lifespan of their entrepreneurial endeavors.

When owners get to the stage of planning to transfer more authority to management, they should be aware that the emotional side of this process is not only long but ubiquitous. Doubts, moments of deep reflection, or other intense reactions affect almost everyone at each stage of the shift. Spirited responses are expected whether owners are just beginning to delegate long-held duties, stepping back from day-to-day management, selling their business, or otherwise exiting from business ownership. And no wonder. Businesses typically absorb a significant part of owners' lives, energy, and resources. And they require the owners—and often their spouses and families—to make great sacrifices, usually over a span of many years. Every stage of business ownership places some stress on owners. It's not surprising that the decision to step away from the day-to-day involvement and, indeed, to sell or transfer the business within a family can be the most draining period of ownership. While all business owners experience emotional stresses that need to be addressed, we've found that family businesses or those with multiple business partners experience additional layers of emotional stress or conflicts that need to be identified and addressed accordingly.

Addressing Owner Fears

One of our main objectives for writing this book was to motivate business owners to view their journey through life not only from the point of view of the business and its success or failure, but also to focus on defining life objectives and aligning the business to help them achieve those goals. That process of alignment is often blocked by the dynamics and psychology of the small- to medium-sized business owner. That blockage usually comes into full display during the succession planning period or the process of shifting out of the day-to-day business activities.

Their anxiety and hesitancy are often rooted in fears. In the earlier chapters, we discussed some of the anxieties and emotions that come into play. We opened the first chapter with the story of Tom, the business owner who was forced to face his feelings of dread when a fellow business owner and friend died suddenly shortly after selling his business, in part because he did not have a plan for life after business ownership. And we revisited the topic of fears in subsequent parts of the book—Gordon, in chapter 2, whose despair over the changing business environment put his financial security at risk. And then, Mary, profiled in chapter 4, whose fear of loss of control almost thwarted her plans to transition management responsibilities and then sell her software business to a handpicked member of her management team.

As these and many other case studies we've shared show, an experienced business transition and exit advisor is crucial in setting a plan that successfully navigates through the changeover process and, in particular, when owners face the intense emotional experiences that are inevitable in each phase of the process. If it is done correctly, facilitation can help address the emotional obstacles and remove or mitigate them to ensure they don't throw the process off track or stop it altogether.

There are many fears related to progressing from ownership to the next phase of one's life that owners are prone to encounter as their roles begin to change. These intense feelings commonly fall into four major categories. First, there's a fear of loss of wealth. Since a business often constitutes the largest part of an owner's holdings, it's natural for them to be concerned that delegating responsibilities—let alone selling the business—will cut off the cash flow.

The concern owners have is twofold. On the one hand, they worry that the investment required to hire additional managers to share the responsibilities may reduce the cash available to them as owners in the short term. On the other hand, they fret about whether they will have financial security after they exit the business whether they sell it to a manager under an installment loan contract or sell it outright to a third party. Owners want to live comfortably and make sure they don't run out of money pursuing the lifestyle they choose following an exit. And in family transfers with a sale and gift aspect, they certainly don't want to end up dependent on their children. This fear of wealth loss often is the major obstacle that dissuades business owners from taking that first step to start their planning on their eventual management transition and exit. And any initial hesitancy to start talking about the planning process can be linked to the fear of losing control over their wealth.

As we discussed earlier in this book, we have assisted our clients by working with owners and their significant others to identify any wealth gap that they may have. There are many ways (tools) that this can be calculated. We customized a personalized What-If Financial Analysis. It is one of the tools business owners can use to focus their financial goals and objectives. We raise the What-If Analysis in the context of this chapter, too, because we have found it to be a useful resource in addressing the fear of loss of wealth. The assessment takes into consideration all of an owner's assets and other sources of income, their current and desired lifestyle spending after they exit from the business, and legacies they want to fund. The analysis calculates what value needs to be taken out of the business both while operating, via retirement investment savings and upon sale and exit to fund their financial objectives. The "What-If" planning aspect allows the calculation to be made based on various potential exit timeline targets. This planning process is usually helpful in demonstrating to the owner and their significant other that if the business plan is executed successfully, they will have enough financial resources to live their chosen lifestyle and fund their other financial goals.

Sometimes, in the course of this analysis, we recommend that owners readjust their initial timetable or lifestyle desires. In the planning process, we ask the owners and their significant others what they would like if they had a magic wand. We then match that up to what is practical, giving their exit timeline and their business's growth potential. For example, one small business owner we worked with had an informal plan to retire in three years. We prepared his What-If Analysis based on the amount of spending he and his wife expected postexit. With our financial analysis, he quickly saw that the year-over-year value increase his business would have to produce over three years to meet their desired lifestyle spending after he exited the business was unattainable. We suggested that they cut back their spending to meet his expected timetable for the sale of the business. Instead, the owner expanded his work horizon to seven years, to give him the needed time to increase the value of the business, in order to live the lifestyle he and his wife wanted.

When the fear of losing wealth is deep-seated, we encourage owners to take a close look at what's behind it. One client we worked with had amassed a net worth of over $50 million but was nonetheless concerned about potentially not having enough. His fear was similar to those who have lived through the Great Recession of 2007 to 2009 or, for earlier generations, through the Great Depression of the 1930s. In these more complicated cases, we sometimes recommend bringing in a trained psychologist or an executive coach with a background in psychology. This is a rare step but can help owners who get stuck on specific deep-rooted emotional issues.

The fear of conflict is another reaction that daunts many business owners. This anxiety emerges particularly when business partners or family members are involved in the business transition process. Craig and Terry, the two brothers and co-owners of the tool die factory we described in chapter 2, illustrate the kinds of problems the fear of conflict can cause. Their trepidation about possible confrontations kept them from addressing the different needs and demands on them as owners and on their family's involvement.

In these cases, we have found that when the parties are clear and transparent about the issues they face or could face, it's possible to overcome the worries they have regarding potential conflict. We often start by showing owners the potential areas of conflict given their set of individual circumstances. We use a graphic to illustrate the point. And for each possible conflict we identify, we include that as an area of concern that needs to be addressed both in their life and business plans. We try to identify specific action steps to analyze, mitigate, and monitor so they can be addressed before they explode into something that will blow the plan for a sale or a transition to management or family off its tracks or put an anchor drag on the movement forward. Explaining the potential conflict possibilities upfront with a reassurance that the solutions can be worked through, even if at times that can be difficult, gives the owners a path to move forward and begin to address them.

We also believe it is important that business partners, family, and nonfamily, understand they have different financial and nonfinancial objectives.

We also believe it is important that business partners, family, and nonfamily, understand they have different financial and nonfinancial objectives. Some may be financially set while others are not. Our goal is to design a plan that gets everybody most of what they want via compromises and to make it known upfront that each of them will not necessarily get everything they want. To manage conflict, it is crucial to put everything that is known on the table at the initial personal planning stage. There are times when each partner's objectives are so far apart that staying together may no longer make sense. In some family transitions, the kids sometimes don't want to be involved with the business or can't work with one sibling or another. It's better to acknowledge situations like this now rather than later. The option of one or more of the partners selling should be put on the table. And family businesses should look to other alternatives rather than trying to force family involvement when it appears untenable.

Even though some feelings may be bruised, the solution usually prevents the situation from exploding into anger, despair, heated conflict, lost opportunity, and financial loss.

The story of Joe, whom we worked with to transfer his business to his children, is an excellent example of a fear of conflict in a situation we encountered and how we dealt with it. Joe owned the business, and both he and his wife had been active in it. The couple built the company from scratch to the stage when annual revenues exceeded $5 million and the business was financially successful. Their two adult sons had worked in the business through high school, college, and immediately after college, so they had a good understanding of the business generally but had not been trained to operate it strategically. One obstacle was that Joe was not a good communicator and ran the company in an authoritarian manner. Different advisors had come and gone. We were the third set of advisors invited to help. In a private meeting, the sons warned us that they had been going to family counseling with a psychologist, and he had kicked them out, saying he couldn't help them. They wished us luck.

Aware of these challenges, we set up rules of engagement that all the parties had to follow. It was important in these meetings that they addressed each other in a businesslike fashion as owner-employee, manager-employee, and not parent-child or child-parent. We also made sure to anchor the end goal that Mom, Dad, and the sons wanted—to pass on the ownership of the company in a couple of years if the kids hit certain operational and management milestones during a two-year coaching period. We facilitated the execution of the strategic plan with the four of them in monthly meetings. We accomplished a lot. When conversations started getting louder and heated, we referred to the rules and worked to bring them down. In the instances where there were heated exchanges, we would begin the next meeting by bringing up the last meeting's conflict, the end goal we were all trying to reach, the disruption it caused in moving forward, and ways to better present differences of opinion to keep the peace, build better relationships, and get to the finish line.

One day when the four of them came into the conference room, we placed a stuffed skunk on the table. They looked at the skunk, then at us, and then back to the skunk. After a few silent moments, we told them that one of our former partners compared the tough conversations that no one wanted to broach to the way people avoided skunks. "Well, it's obvious we have a problem that needs attention, so I've got to put the skunk on the table," he'd say. And then, we would proceed to address what the issue was. We then brought up our skunk issue at hand—the strained and sometimes heated exchanges they'd been having were disruptive, unproductive, and emotionally draining on all parties. In going forward, we asked them to refer to any issues/

concerns they have as skunk issues and not individual personal issues. By not pointing fingers and making them personal, our survival fight-or-flight impulse doesn't kick in, and emotions, for the most part, are usually tempered.

It turned out that the skunk metaphor worked well, and we experienced fewer crises. In the end, the sons' two-year milestone was completed, the financial arrangements were put in legal documents, and ownership was transferred to them. By the end of the fourth or fifth year, the team of two sons completed the strategic plan we put together, revenues more than doubled, and income was at all-time highs. The conflict was ever-present during the transition process, but acknowledging the challenges going into it allowed us to plan and navigate through them and get to the finish line and beyond successfully.

The loss-of-control fear is yet another widespread issue. It often makes owners anxious about whether they should entertain the process of selling or otherwise exiting the business at all. One of the major drivers propelling the loss-of-control fear is the feeling owners have that no one can run the business as well as they can, and if they weren't there, it would fail. Through discussion, we can demonstrate that with proper oversight and financial reporting, there could be significant growth potential by giving others in the organization the opportunity to take over some of the critical responsibilities and decisions that owners otherwise want to hold onto.

When Mary, the business owner we profiled in chapter 4, showed the signs of not wanting to give up control, our conversations focused on the advantages of giving some of those duties to others in the organization. Engaging managers in the day-to-day running of the business frees owners up to pursue other activities while also enhancing the business's value. Like in most things, proper leverage is the key to tremendous success.

As part of coaching owners to deal with the fear of losing control, we show them that by accepting things being done a little less "perfect" than what they could do themselves and leveraging others to share in the tasks, much more can be done. Those changes could provide owners with even greater strategic control than they had versus dealing with all the daily fires themselves.

Perhaps the most common and challenging fear owners face is the fear of change. Owning a business often requires owners to follow a strict lifestyle routine. When faced with the prospect of changing that lifestyle, owners tend to have one of three reactions. Some are excited to move on and not be tied to the business anymore. They are ready to experience new things, such as spending more time with family and friends, traveling, getting back to hobbies they haven't had time for, etc. Others are simply reluctant to consider leading a different lifestyle or even making minor adjustments. Let's face it, most people don't like change, period! And then, there's the group in between—owners who are open to trying a few things out—trial runs if you will, hobbies, volunteer groups, other business opportunities, to see what feels right. Our facilitation here is typically centered around awareness of options they should be thinking about based on our many years of case history experience and the experiences of other advisors in the field. We act sometimes as a sounding board and, at different times, as the devil's advocate.

Suppose a changeover in ownership of a family business drags on because Dad or Mom has a tough time making that change commitment and can't let go. In that case, we as advisors might need to sit the owner down and let them know that their son Little Johnny is now fifty and needs to start making plans to take care of his own family and not be dependent on them.

What happens if Johnny walks away from the business? Worse yet, what happens if he leaves the business, and he opens something up on his own, and employees and customers leave with him? Frank and honest conversations are needed at this point. And take it from us, no matter how supportive the older generation is to transition controls and ownership to the younger generation, there are times when the fear of change puts a chokehold on them. This is the time that an experienced advisor is invaluable to help them work through it.

In the course of evolution in business ownership, the emotional challenges surface constantly, but they typically hit owners hardest during two different periods. Many owners experience the emotional barriers in the early planning stage. The fears that emerge in this phase are usually unspoken and often deter owners from taking any planning steps, until something emotional hits them and spurs them into action. In cases where the owner fails to address a particular fear early in the process entirely, one thing is for sure—they don't simply go away. The same fears are likely to return and intensify when trying to transition to the graduate level of business ownership and/or as they come closer to the time they leave the business.

One Owner's Emotional Journey

The issues that faced Daniel—the visionary software owner—give a good insight into what many owners can expect as they work through the process and timeline of stepping back from the day-to-day selling or otherwise exiting their business. As we detailed in the previous chapter, Daniel's approach to two decades of business ownership, including the control he took over the timing of the sale of his business and to whom, was, in many ways, exemplary. He trusted his instincts, was flexible, and turned to us for advice and guidance when he felt it was needed.

Daniel's emotional reactions centered on the fear of loss of control. He actually experienced it long before he gave the green light to begin the negotiations to sell his business. When Daniel was nearing sixty, pressure and expectations around him began to mount.

Financial advisors, friends, and even some family members sounded the same message: maybe it was time to sell the company and retire. Daniel listened and struggled with the messages he was getting for some time. At times he thought perhaps they were right. At other times, he felt a strong desire to continue to build the company. That internal struggle continued until the day came when Daniel took a bold stand. "I'm not going to sell because someone tells me it is time," he said. "I will do it my way and on my terms." And with that, he was free of that particular struggle and was able to march on.

Several years later, when Daniel was ready to approach a potential sale, he did so initially with a sense of curiosity. "Will a third-party offer finally validate the value I believe we've built here?" he asked, hoping somehow that he could control that outcome too and by doing so secure the future of the enterprise he had built over the past two decades. Additionally, one other critical component he wanted control of—as is true for many business owners—was the future of his team. He wanted to make sure that any new owner would take care of them. He hoped that they would, if possible, receive better opportunities than the ones he could have provided for them if he continued to own the company. So even as he was contemplating selling and moving on, he continued to try and extend his control.

Daniel's experience is an example of how the fear of losing control manifests itself at different times. Once the bargaining began in earnest, Daniel experienced another set of emotional responses. The buyer made an agreeable offer, including terms that would reward those employees who stayed on, and the parties then moved on to the due diligence phase. Even though Daniel loved data and details and relied heavily on advisors, this stage of the process was emotionally taxing. The actual process of selling a business tends to be a distraction to the ordinary operation and management of the company, and as a result, other projects fall through the cracks. The same was the case here also. It seemed that Daniel was working eighty hours a week trying to oversee operations while also conducting due diligence reviews.

The intrusive nature of the due diligence process also raised the issue of whom to tell in the organization and when. In Daniel's case, there were only a few members of the senior management staff who knew what was going on. And Daniel made sure to keep it that way. And that, in turn, added another layer of emotional stress. Keeping the pending sale of a business secret to allow most employees to focus on the tasks at hand is a personal choice some owners make. There are pros and cons to both approaches, but in general, it is helpful to have some people in the know to assist the owner with the tasks involved in selling a business. In any case, owners should be aware of the tensions they will inevitably face, so they are not surprised when under the due diligence gun.

When the due diligence process was complete, and the buyer felt comfortable with the financial information provided to him for his offer, Daniel and his team entered one of their most emotional phases. Daniel had to come to terms with the fact that the sale was likely going to happen. With the stated objective of protecting the future of the company and its legacy, Daniel wanted to control the business strategies that would be implemented once ownership had transferred to the new buyer. As his attempts to dictate the buyer's actions posttransaction fell short, at least twice, Daniel almost pulled out of the deal. It was time for us to have one of those frank conversations to remind him that when a buyer purchases a business, they earn the right to do with it as they like, even if it means the result will not work out. It was important for Daniel to know when to stop pushing and come to terms with the original plan and his assessment that it was time for him to move on. He took the business as far as he could take it. Now it needed a much larger entity and funding to carry it forward. After reflection, Daniel was ready to move forward, and he worked with the buyer to set a timetable for closing.

The next period revolved around document reviews, conference calls with attorneys, and final number crunching. The deal was now on a glide path to be completed before the holidays. The morning of closing, Daniel left his house, sharing a touching moment with his wife. She had tears in her eyes—a sign of how emotional and monumental this day would be for them. By 10:00 a.m., all of the parties involved were on a conference call. What happened next resembled a NASA launch countdown. One by one, each representative signaled that their part was right to move toward closing with a Go/No call out. It finally came to Daniel's turn. He sat there for several seconds before finally giving his Go to sign off.

And that was it. Daniel sat silently for a few seconds, then stood and went back to lead a management team meeting. Later in the day, we had a chance to celebrate a bit. Daniel, the competitive athlete, had finally reached the finish line he had envisioned so many years earlier.

Daniel continued to work for the buyer for another year to oversee the shift to new ownership.

As his advisors, we were there to help both Daniel and the new owners in the integration. Daniel's new role was challenging to him. Perhaps it was made more complicated because the new owner was a much larger company with thousands of employees, and as a result, they had a lengthy process of arriving at decisions. For an entrepreneur who had become comfortable with making decisions and controlling every outcome without great deliberation and delay, working in a larger company with its own rules and structures was not at all comfortable or enjoyable. Even reaching the kind of simple conclusions Daniel used to make in minutes now required the bureaucracy of several layers of managers. And, of course, this cumbersome routine brought its share of emotional stress.

Daniel finally announced his retirement a year later in an emotional speech to the team. He discussed how he knew this day would come, but it took him a couple of years to come to terms with it. In the end, he was happy he was able to do it on his terms.

Many business owners may view the emotional journey Daniel went through during his long-planned and well thought-out sale as different from theirs. With a staff of more than one hundred, his multimillion-dollar software company was larger than most. Still, the fears he faced as he left his business—fears of loss of control and change—mirror other business owners' experiences.

The importance of awareness cannot be overstated to ensure that you, the business owner, are not caught by surprise or wonder if the emotions you end up feeling are normal. We have made the case as strongly as possible that as owners work through their transition and exit out of their businesses, emotional stress will surface. We cannot emphasize enough how much more manageable these stresses will be if owners are deliberate about assuming control of the process of evolving away from business ownership and, in particular, taking deliberate steps to prepare for the rush of emotions that will surface. Is worrying about the financial future a significant issue? Is there tension with business partners? Is the fear of loss of control lingering in the mind?

Clarity about which issues may affect them should help the business owner break through the barriers that might keep them from focusing on their plans to transition and exit from their business. And as Daniel's story clearly illustrates, transition planning does not mean an exit is imminent. Daniel's goal was over a twenty-five-year timeline.

In the end, it's a fact of life that exiting a business—no matter how owners go about it—is tough on the emotions. Even business owners who address their fears head on and do all they can to work through them are often emotionally daunted during and after the sale. While the steps we outline here make the process easier, owners will inevitably feel a sense of loss after leaving their business and should anticipate some emotional stress as they move on to the new phase of their life. Even though the stress is inevitable, it helps business owners to know that experiencing an intense feeling of loss is okay and even quite normal. As one of our clients recently said after selling his business, "It was a relief knowing that there was nothing wrong with me and that what I was feeling was a normal part of leaving the business."

> *Clarity about which issues may affect them should help the business owner break through the barriers that might keep them from focusing on their plans to transition and exit from their business.*

CHAPTER SEVEN

Family Business

Addressing Family Dynamics and Conflicts

T hroughout *The Graduate Level of Business Ownership*, we've focused on the various issues that business owners encounter and how they should deal with the related emotional and personal challenges that come throughout the arc of ownership and especially during the transition process. We would be remiss if we didn't note the unique circumstances that family businesses and couples often face. Family—including spouses or significant others, children, and sometimes grandchildren—whether involved in the business or not, play a significant role at times in the actions or lack of action of business owners. Understanding those dynamics can be useful when owners are trying to chart a way forward for the business and for themselves. These circumstances and potential conflicts intensify when family members and couples are involved in the business. If the conflicts are not addressed properly, the fallout can cost more than just the loss of the business.

A Typical Family Business

One good case in point is the MacArthur family, which grappled with the gamut of emotional issues. The parents, Benedict and Leslie, both in their late sixties, owned a machine parts business in Northern California for twenty-five years. Their adult children, Marvin, thirty-seven; Lisa, thirty-five; Jen, thirty-three; and Dirk, twenty-seven, were working in the business at different levels. Lisa started part time when she was in college, came fully on board after graduation, gradually took over management responsibilities from her father, and eventually became general manager. Marvin had begun working in the business a couple of years after Lisa. While Lisa focused on overseeing the office, Marvin was often out in the field, interfacing with clients. Jen and Dirk joined the business a decade or more after Lisa, and by that time the two older siblings had developed a good system of collaborating together. Due to the age gaps and lifestyle differences, the younger siblings had a tougher time establishing a comfortable working rapport with the older two.

In their initial estate planning, developed many years previously, the parents had given the oldest three children varying percentages of nonvoting shares in the company: Marvin, 32 percent; Lisa, 35 percent; and Jen, 6 percent. Dirk had no shares. The plan was for the remaining shares, which belonged to the father, to be distributed to the four children as part of his transition and exit from the business. When the family asked for our assistance, the father had already told the children he was going to gift the remaining shares to them, but he never went through with the execution of transferring the shares.

Once we met with the MacArthurs, we quickly discovered something that is common in most businesses: the children, like any group of employees, all had different skill sets, work habits, and motivational drives. But in this case the issues and built-in resentments were amplified because of the family dynamics. For one thing, Lisa and Marvin were hard driven and kept their focus on the success of the business, even if it meant sacrificing personal time. For Jen and Dirk, who were of a younger generation, home life and socializing with friends were as important as work. Lisa was at her desk promptly by 7:30 a.m. Jen and Dirk came in at various times throughout the morning.

The parents requested that we structure a succession buyout that met their lifestyle needs. Among our duties was to help guide the family through the transfer of the business from the father to the children and develop a structure of communication that brought all four children into the management oversight loop.

When we began our engagement, the family was already seeking to address some deep- seated issues regarding inclusion, communication, work ethic, and family position. Dirk and Jen, the youngest and more recent family employees, were trying to find their space and where they fit into the company. All four children needed to learn how to work and dialogue together on business issues.

Often what is needed, particularly for new family members who are employees, is training in office etiquette. Daily operations should not be interrupted by inquiry outside each family member's daily responsibilities. We defined this situation as an employee "not swimming in their own lane." This includes asking questions about sales, profitability, general operations, or offering comments on other employees or financial performance. The time and occasion for bringing everyone up to date and sharing insights with full dialog is at monthly strategic management meetings. These meetings should have a fixed agenda with full management reporting of financials, KPI tracking, and so on. Questions and comments can then be brought up and discussed with everyone present instead of one-off conversations with one or two of the other family members throughout the month. And it is imperative that each of them wear a business and not a family hat during these meetings. In other words, they should approach issues from a business and not a family perspective.

One of the initial and biggest causes for conflict we had to deal with was Dirk. His tendency for departing from his defined role as well as other shortcomings became disruptive and led to rifts between the children. Jen was at first supportive of Dirk in trying to work out the issues. Marvin and Lisa, who maintained a sharp interest in the business's profitability, were less tolerant and more critical. The conflicts became the source of time-consuming disputes in the workplace.

As is the case with many family businesses when things go wrong, tensions also surfaced whenever the MacArthurs gathered outside the office. Family gatherings sometimes became unpleasant and awkward. Leslie, like most mothers, attached more importance to family togetherness than business success. Her desire was that all of her children got along and were able to benefit from the fruits of her and Benedict's many years of hard work. The issues at work were not important to her. That stance undoubtedly enabled Dirk's behavior.

Fortunately for us, in their attempts to grapple with interpersonal issues, the family had already enlisted outside help. Stanley, a psychologist, an experienced family business advisor, and an executive coach, had been counseling the family, concentrating on setting boundaries for how they should communicate with one another and other rules of engagement.

We said we were fortunate Stanley was there already because we strongly believe that there comes a time when business advisors have to look in the mirror and realize they alone don't have all the tools to assist everyone. This was one of those cases—where the emotional stresses were sufficiently acute that tackling them was outside of the boundaries of our expertise.

As is our practice when the situation calls for it, we collaborated with Stanley and had several family meetings together. As we outlined our going-forward plan, we took into consideration his observations, concerns, and communication goals.

We came up with a game plan that concentrated on four critical deficiencies we identified. Our initial focus was on developing a plan that would outline the goals and strategies required for the company to maintain sustainability during and after the change of ownership while also addressing the objectives of all of the stakeholders. For Benedict and Leslie, we had another action item—to establish a compensation package that took care of their identified value gap in order to meet their financial lifestyle objectives. Third, as part of the overall succession plan, we sought to set up a program for teaching and coaching Jen and Dirk, the two younger siblings, on business management best practices since they lacked the experience.

Finally, to help the business run more smoothly, we established a platform for the family to communicate on business matters in a way that did not interfere with day-to-day work.

When Family and Business Collide

We successfully ran through several monthly management meetings, and as could be expected, several work-related issues came up, which were addressed adequately in the beginning. As time went on, however, the lack of compatibility of the various family members became more glaring, and the issues became more acute. The problems with Dirk kept resurfacing: not sticking solely to his responsibilities, directing others in the office not under his responsibility, work product shortfalls, and coming in late/leaving early. Ultimately, Dirk was asked to leave. To keep family peace, while we worked out a resolution, the family continued to pay his full benefits. Had Dirk not been a family member, he would likely have been let go a lot sooner. But as we noted earlier, unique circumstances usually surface when there are family members in the business. As a result of this turn of circumstances, our directive took a different turn—negotiating a fair settlement for Dirk to give up his promised ownership with a financial package that was agreeable by all members of the family.

This saga dramatizes one of the most common difficulties family businesses encounter: how to separate the systems that govern the business from those that govern the family. The parents' wish—that the children collaborate in the business together—was unworkable because of incompatibility issues. The MacArthurs' experience further shows the tensions that occur within the family and the workplace when the family is unable to draw lines between the two. In a business, the focus must be targeted on profits, revenues, efficiency, and growth. In a family, the emphasis is on the development and support of family members. It is also common for the rules of dealing with conflict to be very different between a family and the business.

At home, expectations are informal, while in the office rules of conduct are often formalized—even written down—and must be followed strictly for the business's operations to function successfully. In family structures, members are often rewarded for who they are while businesses reward employees based on their performances and penalize them for mistakes. In family businesses, we suggest that procedures for separating the management of family systems from those of the business should be put in place when a family member first joins the business. If the lines are blurred, it will complicate the operations of the business.

Although it was not the case with the MacArthurs, there are other common problems with family businesses we have run across over the years. The first is the timing of the transfer to the next generation. Sometimes parents hold on to control for too long. At other times the children take control before they are fully ready. There are also circumstances when the parents force the children to be involved when they should not or do not want to be involved. Neither of these scenarios is good for the long-term benefit of the business or the individual family members. Finding the right timetable takes work.

The second is the lack of clear communication among all the family stakeholders regarding Mom and Dad's desired plan. Too often the parents make plans for the business' future without discussing it with the kids, or worse yet, without understanding the impact on the business. One case that comes to mind that we were brought into after the event, was where the dad's shares were distributed to his six children upon his death based on how much time they spent with him in his final days and not on whether it was the right thing for the business. In fact as a result, any common business challenge became an argument as the younger ownership group could not make a decision to save their lives.

The third common issue with the transfer of ownership within family businesses has to do with value assigned to the business. On many occasions and in order to make the deal work, the business's value is discounted in family transfers, and the kids are allowed to pay for the transaction over time, from the business's cash flow. In cases like these, the circumstances may not be optimal for business owners who do not want to be financially dependent on their children's success running the business. In such cases, we make sure that the parents' financial plan accounts for the reduced value and the likelihood of receiving cash payments over an extended period of time. Furthermore, we try to be certain that the parents are emotionally prepared for that outcome—not necessarily just the fact they will likely be getting less money, but also the idea of relinquishing control while still being dependent on the business's cash flow. The goal is to head off cases such as a particular one we are aware of where the father and son agreed on the orderly transfer of the business and signed the paperwork, only for Dad to bring in someone the next day to still try to sell the business for a better price.

Avoiding Family Transition Land Mines

Some versions of either the dilemma the MacArthur family faced or the other scenarios we have outlined occur in most family businesses. This mix of thorny issues and the difficulty families have finding solutions may explain why transferring business ownership from one generation to the next often fails and why, at times, the business ends up being sold to an unrelated party instead. According to the Center for Family Business, only 30 percent of family-owned businesses survive into the second generation. Around 13 percent make it to the third generation running things. And only 3 percent succeed in maintaining the business in the family into the fourth generation.[7] These statistics don't necessarily mean that the majority of each generation that takes over the business's reins crashes and burns. The second or later gen-

> *Transferring business ownership from one generation to the next often fails.*

---

7   Conway Center for Family Business, "Family Business Facts," accessed October 2021, familybusinesscenter.com/resources/family-business-facts/.

eration might have continued operating the business successfully but decided it was time to cash out and start doing something else. There are also instances in which some family members put up with other relatives in the business for a while. But later on, they decide they've had enough and believe it best for all involved to sell and split up the proceeds, and for each of them to move on to their own thing. And then there are examples where family members who don't have the same drive, ability, commitment, and perseverance that the previous generations had ultimately fail and go out of business.

If families are going to beat those odds, they must be willing to put in a significant amount of planning and work and seriously consider enlisting the services of an experienced advisor. Too often we find ourselves attempting to fix the problems do-it-yourself business owners got themselves into or being the second or third advisor on the scene to finally deal with the real personal and nonpersonal issues that are part of a transition. Ideally the process should start by asking each side engaged in the process of shifting ownership responsibilities— those taking over the business, and the parents who are hoping to relinquish control to them—to carefully think through the following very important questions.

What parents need to consider regarding the next generation's readiness to take over the family business:

+ Are they ready to take over the day-to-day operations and lead the organization?

+ Do they have the necessary skill set and experience?

+ Can they run the business independently without our day-to-day involvement?

+ Do they understand the obligations and challenges, and are they up to them?

+ Have they been tested under fire?

+ In the case of multiple children, who should ultimately make the final decisions?

+ Do they truly have a passion or burning desire for business?

+ Do they suffer from a false lure of a comfortable life without great efforts or sacrifice?

What the next generation needs to think through when considering taking over the reins of the business:

+ Do they understand Mom and Dad's dependency on the business and their potential need to stay connected to it?

+ Do they grasp the process of knowledge transfer?

+ Do they understand the emotional issues involved in transitioning out of a business? It is not as simple as "up and out."

+ Do they see potential issues working with their parents, other siblings, or managers?

+ What impact will the transition have on customers and the business in general?

+ Do they understand the financial risk they personally and the company will be taking on?

Ultimately, communication and agreements between parents and children should be documented and signed by the parties for both the future leadership succession and future business ownership transfer. This becomes even more important when parents are considering the future of multiple children and their role within the business or those that should remain outside of the family business, for one reason or another. These agreements should stipulate some of the following critical items:

✦ Who will make final decisions and run the company (during the succession process and after the transfer is complete)?

✦ What will be the separate role/responsibilities of each party? Who will determine them?

✦ How will business conflicts be handled?

✦ What is the future leader's vision for the new business and its potential impact on business sustainability?

✦ What will the management structure look like, and who will make that determination?

✦ What is the contingency plan if things don't work out? Do you sell the company?

While these questions are critical to determining the readiness of the next generation, we should not underestimate the complex challenges children face growing up around the business or sharing a home with an entrepreneurial personality. Picture a son or daughter coming into their mom or dad's business as an apprentice and a few years later assuming a leadership role over the very same set of employees. We remember one such son who came back to work for the company after college and found that he had to constantly correct employees to call him James and not Little Jimmy. It's just one of many examples illustrating how tough moving up to a position of leadership in a family business can be for the new generation.

Now imagine what it is like for a son or daughter to live in a house with a business owner who has a dominant personality, perhaps one who was absent for many hours during the day. That child may find it hard to step into the parent's shoes when the time comes or exert the same level of leadership. Some, on the other hand, may flatly reject anything to do with the business or the way their father/mother may have run it. Cases like this do not have to result in the son or daughter disengaging or leaving the business. The right advisor can serve as a mediator between the two generations and set up systems to make the change in ownership work. Remember our story of Mary and Elizabeth, who each had a different management style, but yet were successful in running the business in their own unique way.

The questions we posed above provide a good framework for the conversations that need to take place. It is crucial that each side consider them thoroughly and respond honestly and sincerely. In many cases, the brainstorming and discussions involved—and the answers—will lead the family to conclude that more planning may need to be done in order to successfully proceed with the transition. Alternatively, it could lead to the determination that the planned management and ownership shifts don't make sense to pursue in the present form.

Depending on the deficiencies, various family members may be asked to participate in training, counseling, classes, or other activities to get them fully prepared for the changes in management. The procedures prescribed are often arduous, but following through with them is a key part to successfully executing the process of transferring management from parents to children. It's important to establish milestones that the participants must pass before moving to the next stage. If management training is needed for the children, for example, they must successfully complete each stage of it before proceeding to the next.

One of the strategies we use most frequently with families in business is developing and operating under a set of "Rules of Engagement" when communicating with one another. This exercise trains each member to be clear about which hat they are wearing when they communicate with other family members. Parent-child dialogues differ greatly from owner- management dialogues, even if they involve the same people and are about the same subject.

When all the planning, coaching, and training is completed, the family should have resolved several key issues. The initial and perhaps most important issue is determining whether there is a core group of family members who are willing to make a sincere commitment and have the drive to keep the business running. Secondly, they must determine whether those who would assume leadership of the business are comfortable communicating and working together. Third, as mentioned above, the owners and the inheritors have to agree on a management and ownership transition timetable that works for all parties.

As easy as these decisions sound, each of them may require the family to navigate some complicated emotional mazes. For example, deciding that some of the children or other offspring are suitable to manage the business while others may not be. In cases where the next generation does not stand up to the challenge of commitment or of increased responsibility, or where irresolvable differences surface, it may turn out that selling the business makes better sense than transferring it to the next generation. A lot of parents we have worked with, although not requiring fair market value to be paid, are still dependent on some, if not most, of the proceeds.

To protect their lifestyle, we as advisors need to make sure that the business will be sustainable in order for them to have a better chance of getting paid in full. When that outcome is not clear, the parents must be told that their children don't have what it takes to keep the business running successfully long term, and instead they should consider selling the company to outside buyers. This decision is a hard one for parents to make while still keeping family peace. This highlights the importance of having outside guidance. An experienced advisor can set clear milestones that both the parents and children know have to be reached and without progress, the decision will be made to sell the business to a third party. The advisor will do what is right for the business regardless. Done properly, there should be no surprises if that happens. And Mom and Dad are spared the role of being the bad guys who have to deliver the message.

Returning to the MacArthur family's story, after several weeks of meetings and negotiations with Dirk, the remaining three shareholders, and Mom and Dad, we were able to work out an agreement that everyone thought they could live with. Although there was a split between the family, the MacArthur business succession succeeded.

The agreement allowed the family to get rid of the emotional distractions so that the three remaining siblings could focus exclusively on running the business. With Dirk's departure, the tensions in the office were eliminated. This made way for Lisa, Marvin, and Jeb, with our assistance, to concentrate on developing and executing the future strategic vision plan. The positive results were dramatic. Revenues increased by 30 percent over the next four years, and profitability increased by 400 percent. In our continued engagement with the business, we held regularly scheduled strategic planning meetings a couple of times a year to track progress, make improvements, and plan next steps. Like a trained athlete, successful businesses can benefit from continued coaching.

One important lesson of the MacArthur family story is that family members must perform in family businesses. When they do, it sets the tone for a strong work ethic for the whole company. But perhaps this saga's biggest lesson is that business owners should not put family before sound business practices. Very few parents want to leave any of their children out of their legacy. The planning process can

> *Business owners should not put family before sound business practices.*

identify potential land mines, and the family member can be provided for through other means outside of the business and avoid all of the emotional stress, arguments, and distractions.

When Significant Others View Things Differently

Sometimes rather than parent/children issues in business, issues with changes in the business or the owners' approach to the business may involve the parents themselves. Whether or not one or both partners are engaged in the business, issues often surface. One example is Baxter and Jill. They were both successful in their own right, each with type-A personalities and high energy. They both left senior-level corporate jobs twelve years ago and started a communications company together in Georgia. Both threw themselves into the business, and it took off. After four years of co-ownership, Jill decided to leave the business in order to have more time to look after their two kids. Baxter continued to run the company, and it kept growing. In the past couple of years, Jill wanted her husband to back off work a little, spend more time with her and their kids, and enjoy the fruits that all his years of labor gave them while their children were still at home. He was in agreement with the thought process and verbally supported her goal. He agreed to retain us to help him plan the transition of management responsibilities to take a lesser role that didn't demand as much of his time.

We started personal objectives planning with the couple, and in the course of it, we discovered that the two of them had significantly different value drivers. Jill's top driver was family. She felt that shifting time and attention away from the business and toward family pursuits was important especially because the business was on a steady growth path. For Baxter, family was important, too. But it was his secondary value driver. His primary driver was accomplishment. As long as he stayed energized in the business, it felt right to him to keep the running of the company as a priority. That was his source of fulfillment and what fed his energy. In our value and objectives report, we addressed these differences. We stated that their primary goal was to spend more time with each other and the family, because deep down they both still wanted that. However, we also pointed out that this wasn't going to happen without great effort on the husband's part, and they both needed to know that.

Because the husband wasn't wired to take the necessary steps naturally, it had to be pointed out to him that to make it happen he would need to commit to considerable work and effort to change his dream. The wife also needed to have clarity about it so she would not be continually disappointed if her husband was unable to successfully execute the necessary corrective steps to change. There were tears from both sides as they came to realize that what we had observed was exactly where they were. The result was not quite where they wanted to be. Nevertheless, it was important that this difference was recognized to avoid conflict later when their stated expectations were not met.

Many of the differences couples face are small wrinkles that are easy enough to work out. But sometimes the gaps are wider. One partner might envision moving away from and eventually exiting out of a business as the time to live more luxuriously, while the other imagines a simpler life. One might be geared up to devote his or her spare time to philanthropic activities while the other wants to spend more time with the children, grandchildren, and other family members. One might want to start a new business while the other sees this as the chance to be free of business worries.

Communication problems are what often causes these differences. One partner assumes the other knows what they are thinking, because of all the years they have lived together and have talked about things generally. But those conversations usually involve a kind of half listening in which certain key nuances are brushed over, and important details are not processed.

Another reason that two partners sometimes harbor differing dreams that they have a tough time expressing is rooted in fears. Just as fears keep business owners from focusing on leaving the business, so too do they sometimes keep family or couples from engaging together in open discussions about their personal dreams. With couples, the fear of conflict is one that often comes into play. One or the other partner or both may fear that the harmony or balance they have become comfortable with over the years could easily unravel when they begin to talk of entering another phase of life.

Even in cases where both partners thought they had an understanding about how they would spend their life in the post-business-ownership era, they sometimes learned that their interpretations of what was discussed were actually different. A funny example of this is David and Lila, who ran a business together. They owned a chain of pharmacies that they hoped one day would be transferred to their son. When they discussed life post business ownership in our financial planning session of what they would need to support their future lifestyle, they independently answered that they'd like to travel across the US. But when we asked for details on that dream during our meeting together, Lila said she loved camping out and looked forward to it. David, in contrast, pictured the two moving about in higher-end hotels.

Whatever the background of couples or the particular emotional hurdles they encounter, the goal is the same: to come up with and execute a transition plan in which both partners can realize their dreams or at least realize some of them. Just like with transfers of ownership and/or management in family businesses, getting to that stage is far easier with the help of an outside advisor. An advisor can guide the couple toward compromise solutions. For example, David's interest in staying in hotels versus Lila's preference for camping was compromised in a way that satisfied both parties: an agreement they would buy a Winnebago. Other times there might be differences that are much farther apart that might require further conversation by the couple to try and work through, either on their own or with outside counseling. But let's face it, couples are not always in agreement, so there are times when they just let things sit as they are. While that is by no means a perfect situation, sometimes it's good enough. And in our context, that's all that really matters as we help them plan their eventual transition and exit out of the business and walk toward their next phase of their lives together.

One point we have made throughout the book bears reiterating here: whether they are part of a family, in a relationship, or solo, business owners should start their planning as early as possible. That sets them up for the smoothest transitions. But we acknowledge that there are occasions when circumstances do not always allow advance planning, or owners have deliberately put planning off, and a sudden, unexpected exit is mandated. In the next chapter, we will discuss situations when owners are confronted with such circumstances.

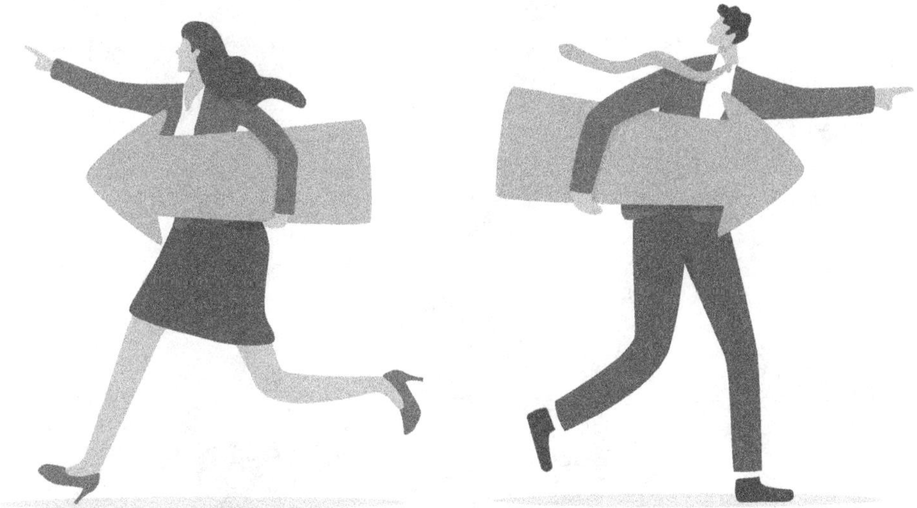

CHAPTER EIGHT

When the Unexpected Happens

How to Plan an Exit When Time Is Limited

H opefully by now you realize and agree with us on the importance of entrepreneurs controlling their destiny early on in the arc of business ownership, and doing so with proper planning that lays out a path to achieve their personal goals and objectives. This path would then be supported by business strategies that include greater profitability, business value growth, and planning for the eventual exit from their business, whether planned or unexpected due to disability or premature death. We also detailed the action items owners can and should take to prepare the business—and themselves—to operate the company successfully, action steps that not only reap the best return on their investment but also meet both the owner's short-term and long-term needs and those of their family members. Our profiles of various business owners who have gone through careful planning and diligent execution of both an operating and exit plan illustrate that the transition process typically extends over years and often over more than a decade.

While our advocacy for thoughtful and long-term business exits is unequivocal, we know that in some cases circumstances do not always give business owners the opportunity for them to properly plan, while in other cases some owners are just unwilling to put in the time and effort of advance planning. In either case, unfortunately, sometimes—for numerous unforeseen circumstances—owners need or want to exit their business on a short timeline. Even given a short time frame to implement a transition, there are steps owners in this situation can and should take to better their current financial position and minimize any disruptions their departure might bring.

Sometimes Life Dictates a Need for Immediate Action

The reasons business owners exit on a shorter-than-optimal timeframe vary widely, but they tend to fall into two broad categories. The owners in the first group find they have little choice but to exit due to unexpected illness or death or other emergency events in the business or with the owner or with someone in their family. Sudden events occur, usually catching everyone with their guard down: the owner suffers a heart attack, a fire or natural disaster destroys the building, a spouse or life partner falls ill or dies, or any number of such catastrophes. Tragically, when dealing with life-threatening family illnesses, the business's monetary value loses its importance, and time becomes the more important currency. For non-life-threatening circumstances, even if there might be ways to salvage the business, they are monumentally challenging, difficult, and/or overly costly. In either case, an immediate exit seems like the only option.

The second category is composed of owners who have, for one reason or another, made a conscientious decision to seek a short-term exit. Many find they have reached their sixties or seventies without having taken the time to evaluate their business, reinvent its purpose, and/or create a path for growth. And they don't want to invest the four to five years that such a process likely requires. Other owners in this group might be at any age but wake with the feeling that they have simply had enough of the business and want to find a way out sooner rather than later. Or perhaps issues surface between business partners or an owner and their spouse that prompt an unplanned exit.

The COVID-19 pandemic, with all its challenges and heightened risks, pushed many business owners into either one category or the other of owners seeking an early exit. In some cases, the loss of business or health issues related to COVID-19 left them with no choice but to exit. In other instances, the challenges imposed by the pandemic were more than owners wanted to shoulder. They didn't want to take the time or effort to build their revenues back up, or they didn't have the ability to hang on until the business environment got back to normal. The crisis drained them of financial resources and the energy to persevere through the hard aspects of business ownership.

Although owners in the two categories are ultimately in the same predicament—seeking a short-term exit—one key difference between them is the amount of time they have to organize and complete an exit. Owners faced with an urgent exit usually have a very tight window—a matter of months or sometimes even less—to organize and execute a sale or transfer or to wind the business down in order to protect the financial assets for their family. Owners in the second category potentially can extend their time horizon with the help of a clear and better path forward. This benefit and difference in the length of time available for executing a plan is invaluable. Depending on which category owners fall into, they should take different approaches and strategies to maximize their financial outcome, given the limited time horizon. We'll explore those differences in just a moment.

> *Our surveys indicate that over 60 percent of owners have no formal plan at the time they are ready to exit.*

But first, discussing the things that business owners in both categories have in common should also be instructive. For one, all owners who are exiting in a short window should be concerned. If you as a business owner are among those who find the need or desire for an immediate exit—whether it's an urgent exit or one with a bit more time—there is good reason to feel anxious. In our experience, owners of all ages and focuses—software entrepreneurs, car dealership proprietors, and everything in between—have found themselves in similar situations. Our surveys indicate that over 60 percent of owners have no formal plan at the time they are ready to exit. Although this percentage has declined in the past few years, due to education, the increasing awareness of owners as a result of the media's attention on the aging boomer population and as they approach their sixties or seventies, it is still significant. For any business owner with an exit on the horizon and no plan for it in the works, feeling the pressing need to address the short time horizon can be helpful.

Second, urgency should drive owners into action. Whatever the reason owners have for an immediate exit, they should still by all means formulate a game plan. Devising an effective plan under a tight deadline is an occasion where professional guidance is crucial. Our experience working with owners who seek an exit in a shorter time frame shows that having a structured thought process always puts them in a better position. If they at least put something into play, they will almost certainly be able to have a more stable exit and may even be able to receive some value from the business that they would otherwise risk if they rushed through without a plan or by simply closing the doors. Although the circumstances are not ideal, taking certain steps will help owners not only increase the value they'll receive for the business but also might fulfill other objectives.

Just like longer exit plans, short term exits are best when they are tailor-designed to suit the individual business owner's needs, as best it can, given the specific timeline limitations. Regardless of the circumstances of a transition, business owners are unique, and even short-term emergency plans need to be constructed accordingly.

Third, owners with limited time should be aware that their options are likely to be limited as well. For sure, those owners who end up exiting the business in a limited time frame will lose out on the many advantages gained through long-term planning. Above all, they will have less leverage in negotiating an exit deal. They will also have limited opportunity to address the emotional aspects of transition, and little to no time to plan their life after exiting the business. With a short window, owners will also be more restricted in their ability to take control of the transition and their destiny. As we've illustrated throughout this book, when owners give themselves the appropriate time for an exit, they have the time and opportunity to understand value gaps; to build and manage business value; to identify failure points in the business and fix them; and to make personal preparations for the transition. Daniel, the owner we profiled in chapter 5, had utilized all of these advantages and others. He engaged in a long-term exit strategy and was in a position to say no to lucrative offers and chart his business legacy.

We cannot overstate the impact of losing those benefits, some of which are measured in terms of the decreased salability of the business, decreased value, and the emotional toll business owners may face, which is harder to quantify but is just as important to address. Owners who exit in a short window must come to terms with those potential risks.

Executing a Plan with Limited Time and Limited Options

The experience of Jackson—a North Carolina business owner who had to pursue a sudden, unexpected exit—offers insight into the issues that arise in such cases and how they can be addressed. Jackson had owned The Kitchen Sink, a company that provided restaurant supplies nationwide, for twenty years when the COVID-19 pandemic hit, causing the entire restaurant industry, including his business, to take a sharp dive. The sudden loss of income meant that Jackson quickly fell behind on payments. Leading up to this turn of events, Jackson had been transitioning out of his business by bringing on a COO who could have been a potential buyer of the business. The COO's personal finances at this time prevented that from happening. Then COVID hit, essentially shutting down the business. There was no longer a profitable operating business to sell. With no scenario in sight for a rebound of the restaurant sector, Jackson's only viable option was an immediate exit to minimize his losses. He called us to assist him with a plan.

After our initial conversations, we did a review of The Kitchen Sink's financial situation, including debt service, expected miscellaneous revenue stream, cash flow, debts, and an assessment of equipment and inventory market values. We also discussed what Jackson wanted to achieve most in the exit. A conscientious owner, he stipulated that one big priority for him was paying off or at least paying something to his trade creditors. Another was taking care of the bank, which had a secured loan on all of the company's assets and the real estate that he owned personally and rented to the business.

Jackson's assets included a stockpile of restaurant equipment and around $500,000 in advanced payments from companies he had been working with. We laid out a plan that included a couple of steps. The first was to contact a neighbor in the industrial park where he operated his business, who over the years had expressed an interest in the building, to try to expedite a quick sale. That would keep Jackson from having to put the building on the open market, a sales process that could take months to complete. Such a quick deal would also minimize Jackson's monthly bank debt shortfalls.

Step two was to try and coordinate a sale of the assets before the real estate deal closed to pay off the business's secured debt with the bank. In keeping with our charge to organize as efficient and orderly an exit as possible, we proceeded to package what remained of The Kitchen Sink into a bundle. We then sought out candidates who might be in a position to purchase the whole package rather than selling individual assets. But Jackson reached a deal on the real estate and signed an agreement quicker than expected. With time running out to sell the other assets as a bundle, he then sold the assets off individually to the various companies that had expressed an initial interest.

In many ways, Jackson's case was typical of those business owners who are faced with an urgent early exit. Most importantly, the objective of his exit was to address the owner's financial debt and obligations and allow him to transition with a minimal amount of stress, pain, and financial loss. In longer, more strategic transitions, the exit plan often involves addressing issues in the business and maximizing its value to negotiate a higher price. But there was no time for that. Instead, our singular focus was on minimizing Jackson's outstanding bills and seeing him through the exit process. The peculiarities of Jackson's business and circumstances further illustrate how every business is different and must have its own individually designed plan.

Doing the Best You Can with What You Have

Owners who fall into the second category—opting for an exit in a short time frame as opposed to being forced to exit immediately— usually have a bit more flexibility than owners in emergencies like Jackson's. But to make full use of their potentially broader range of options, there are certain steps that they should take.

In particular, they must explore two key aspects of the business. Both paths of discovery are important in determining which options are available for an exit and what is the best one for the owner to take.

Before taking the initial steps of planning a short-term strategy to exit the business, owners should determine whether they need to immediately monetize what they can (versus immediately exiting), or do they have the time to monetize the business over an extended period of time as they transition out of the business.

If as a result of that determination it is found that an owner has the flexibility of time, they can positively impact the business's value or at least maintain it by structuring it to operate without them. As you recall from chapter four, when trying to monetize a business, it can be worth more if it operates independently of the owner. So correcting dependency issues can go a long way in ensuring a positive outcome, whether an owner's time span is months or longer.

The COVID-19 pandemic provided a new sense of urgency for owners to review, or prepare for the first time, continuity plans, because of the grave health uncertainty, and the risk they may not survive was very real to them. So in this case, the need for action wasn't driven by an actual personal event, but the very real threat of something terrible potentially happening. Such plans were driven solely on the determination of how dependent the business was on the departing owner while also attempting to clarify who would step in and perform the necessary tasks if the owner fell ill or died.

There are other circumstances, such as family emergencies, when an owner may feel the need to leave the business in short order, without having to immediately monetize the business. In such cases, having a viable continuity plan could provide a path for an early transitioning out of day-to-day involvement, while the business operates with the support of a good management team. Additionally, a continuity plan can provide an option for an owner to still own the business and receive wages while someone else is running it until he/she decides to monetize it under better circumstances or timing or to step back in if they desire to do so.

The second action item for those who are looking to increase their business's value given the circumstances of a short time frame, is to conduct an operational analysis from a fresh third-party outsider perspective. This kind of close look at the status of the business focuses on areas of strength and weakness, resources available, assessment of management and staff, different service or product revenue streams, and the gross profit performance of each.

Unlike the extensive review discussed in chapter three, the main objective now is to only ascertain what can be done given the specific time frame that could increase or at least maintain value. The strategic action steps, in this case, are completely different from the longer-term value growth planning because the latter needs financial investment and time to execute it. Deploying any of the long-term strategies in haste, just to do something, would be a waste of time, resources, and money at a time when preservation and lower risk strategies are called for. If time allows, this analysis should pinpoint which aspects of the business can be fine-tuned or changed to increase revenues and profitability to increase the business's value upon sale.

Aside from the proactive initiatives and analyses owners should take, there are strategies that business owners on a short-term exit plan should not pursue. They should not start things that won't have the time to fully develop over a short horizon and blossom into a return—such as new product development or acquiring a new business. Such ventures would not only likely be a waste of time and money, but they could also hurt the current value, and bring on extra expenses.

Stick to the Script

As we have noted, every business, business owner, and exit plan is different. An examination of the case of Mitchell offers some per-spective into what was possible for one business owner who had a bit more flexibility but opted to close in a limited time frame. Mitchell approached us because the lease on his company's building, Mitchell's Place, a widget factory, was ending in two years. At sixty-two, after twenty-five years in business, Mitchell decided the expiration of the lease was an opportune time to sell. We started with a detailed business diagnostic questionnaire, which included a deep dive into his financial status, pricing process, and the adequacy of its supply chain.

Based on the information Mitchell provided, we prepared a plan for enhancing the value of his business in preparation for a sale. The plan focused on ways the business could (1) maintain and, if possible, increase its sales in more profitable areas; (2) improve its gross profit by setting up/fine-tuning processes and systems on the shop floor, tracking their key performance metrics, establishing daily short quarterback meetings so everyone was on the same page as to the day's schedule and target objectives, etc.; (3) reduce waste and inefficiencies in the company's system; and (4) review every expense for necessity versus "nice to have." In each of these areas, we pinpointed specific action items for Mitchell to pursue. If these were executed successfully, we believed that they would add value to the business and better position it for a sale.

Mitchell followed diligently through the transition procedures we recommended. As a result, the business rebounded significantly by every metric. From 2016—when we first began working with Mitchell, until 2019—the company's revenue increased by 25 percent, gross profit rose by .4 percent but more importantly net income quadrupled. With this across-the-board positive showing, the business was in a good position for a sale.

Encouraged by the upswing in business, Mitchell decided to put his exit plans on hold and instead push forward with his business and negotiated a month-to-month lease with the building's owner. Mitchell's Place continued on an upward growth path until the COVID-19 pandemic hit. With sales sagging again, Mitchell contacted us to revisit plans for an exit. This time the economy, weakened by COVID-19, added further complications to the potential sale. Mitchell's case is a good illustration of how circumstances can change for owners pursuing an exit, either in the business or the economy or both. The story also offers a lesson: once a plan is formulated, owners are usually best off sticking with the script.

> *Once a plan is formulated, owners are usually best off sticking with the script.*

Navigating a Changing Scenario

Even when owners have the intention of planning an exit early, various factors can emerge and alter the course or pace of the plan. Cindy and Mark's case is an excellent example. They owned a small second-generation grocery store chain in California and reached out to us to help develop an exit strategy for their business. The company was very profitable and provided the couple a great lifestyle. They were in their early sixties and had raised two daughters—including one who worked part time in the business—who were adults and living on their own. They wanted to transition and exit the business in two years to enjoy the fruits of their hard work while they were young and in good health.

We began the process by meeting with them to gain a thorough understanding of their value drivers, their primary nonfinancial objectives, and what they needed financially from the sale to live the financial lifestyle they wanted. During our discussions, we discovered that like many owners of second-generation family businesses, they had mixed emotions about selling and leaving the company.

As we have emphasized throughout the book, selling a business involves various emotions that must be addressed and planned for. In cases like Mark and Cindy's, where there is a family history in the business, a sale becomes a much harder and more emotional event.

During our objectives planning, we talked about the different kinds of buyers and how each would price the opportunity. We compared those potential options to the control and say Cindy and Mark would have on key issues such as how operations continued, employee retention, and timing of events. We also explored the possibility of their children coming into the business full time to take over operations. At the time, that wasn't a viable possibility.

Although both daughters had worked in the business growing up, neither was interested nor had the business management background to ensure the long-term sustainability of the business. Besides, one of the daughters had moved to New York. So the couple decided to sell the business on the open market.

Once we completed the personal objectives stage, we started our operational analysis. That included our business diagnostic–SWOT analysis, described in other areas of this book. We then came up with a strategic plan with specific action steps that could be executed within the two years to increase the business's profitability and enhance its value. At that point we would assist in putting the company up for a sale. When we presented the improvement plan, we learned that Mark had been diagnosed with a health issue that wouldn't allow him to devote the kind of energy needed over the next two years to increase the business's value. Cindy would now have to handle both responsibilities and help with Mark's care.

The couple decided not to wait and asked for our assistance in organizing the sale of the company. Initial interest was strong, and one potential buyer offered a premium price. But then, the COVID-19 pandemic struck, and once again plans changed. All of the prospective buyers moved to the sidelines to wait for COVID-19 to play out. We took a time-out from pursuing buyer candidates.

During that period, Susan, the couple's older daughter, relocated from the East Coast to California to help them out. She joined her sister, Evelyn, who had been working part time in the business. Motivated by the emotional desire to keep a business going that had been in the family for over four decades, there was discussion that instead of the sale, Susan, with Evelyn's assistance, might take over the management of the business.

Shortly thereafter, merger and acquisition activity started picking up again, and a buyer made a solid offer that met the couple's financial objectives. At this stage, the emotional aspects of the transition entered high gear with the emotions of each of the four family members coming into full play. Adding to the complexity was the commitment Susan had made to sell her and her husband's home in New York and relocate to California to come and be part of the family business.

Cindy was at a crossroads and asked if I could come back in to meet with her daughters and help her and Mark make a decision. She was understandably emotionally strained. Not only were they potentially selling the family business, but now her daughters and their futures hung in the balance.

In family transition situations, we always talk separately with the children interested in going into the business so there's no pressure with the parents being present. The children need to know from an independent third party what's expected of them and what's being put at risk for both themselves and their parents.

We met with the daughters and discussed their dad's health and their backgrounds, their business management ability, their desire to get back into the business and take over management responsibilities, and lastly their parents' financial need for them to purchase the business to become owners. We discussed Mom and Dad's financial situation and their underlying objective of having the financial freedom to do what they want, when they want, so that they could enjoy their leisure time together for as long as Mark's health held out. Without a third-party sale, that wouldn't be possible for them.

During the meeting with the daughters, they suggested the potential of running the business for a couple of years to make the suggested value improvements so Mom and Dad received more money. We explained that more money shouldn't be the decision-making driver. It was much more important for Mark and Cindy—and indeed the whole family—to have time to spend together. Additionally, the offer on the table exceeded their parents' financial needs. As we talked, the daughters realized that an outside sale was in their parents' best interest. It was a painful decision for the daughters but one they accepted. The couple then joined us, and we shared the emotional conversations we had with the daughters and the conclusion that they agreed that a sale was in the best interest of the family. As part of the sale agreement, an employment agreement was reached with the buyers for Susan and Evelyn to maintain the family connection to the business.

There are two key insights in Cindy and Mark's story. The first is that business owners should be adamant in sticking with the initial plan when its objectives have been reached even though there may be emotional tugs toward doing something different. And the second is that owners must be willing to meet adversity with agility to move on to the next new options, rather than stopping and calling it quits. In the course of following through with their exit plans, Mark and Cindy had at least five resets and misfires because of changing circumstances. But they persevered! Of course, having an experienced advisor to get them around and through the land mines certainly helped.

In the end, this case brings us back to our original position: business owners should start early in developing an exit strategy. If they fail to do so, they will find themselves grappling to exit in a short time frame. And that's when things can easily get messy.

CHAPTER NINE

Living Your Dreams

*The Ultimate Discovery of Meaning and
Achieving Personal Happiness*

W e have devoted *The Graduate Level of Business Ownership* to prescribing the full scope of formulas and explanations for the best practices business owners should take in running a successful business, building value, living a more fulfilling life, and eventually transitioning from daily hands-on management to a potential exit. Our goal in writing this book was to draw from our experiences with hundreds of business owners and their businesses and answer the essential questions most of them had: What constitutes a successful business? What are other business owners doing? How can the business work for me instead of the other way around?

We hope we have accomplished that goal by approaching these what and how questions from every angle—from the right way to start and think about your business, to how to grow it and make sure it is not dependent on you, to the ways you can live a well-balanced life, and finally to the possibility of exiting your business on your terms and your timetable. As a society, we often evaluate business success by how big or profitable it is or how much money you are able to sell it for. The reality is much simpler. It boils down to whether business owners can live their dreams and fulfill their life objectives. Those are the ultimate success criteria for any owner.

> *It boils down to whether business owners can live their dreams and fulfill their life objectives.*

This final chapter will explore two remaining questions of crucial relevance that business owners ask: When should I start? And what should I do first, particularly as I think about exiting from the business. On one level, the answer to when to engage in proper planning is simple. As we have noted earlier in the book, every business owner will eventually exit, either standing up or going out feet first. And, of course, it's undeniably preferable to exit with a plan than without one.

As a business owner, your desire to engage in this process and take advantage of the benefits of planning your destiny is the key element to make all of this a reality. We simply don't want you to be one of those owners who wakes up to this need only when something terrible happens. We would much rather you do it because you finally have the people power and management processes in place that allow you to be able to take three, four, five weeks or more off every year. Sometimes, it's easier to consider things if you start with the idea that you are no longer there.

What the Other Experts Say

But why should an owner engage in business planning according to the prescriptions we have offered? It's simple: our methodology process has a proven track record. We encourage owners that perhaps the most important reason is to pursue something bolder and more essential than living for their business. We're seeking to help them approach starting and running a business, progressing later to the graduate level of business ownership and their eventual exit from the business as an opportunity to plan their lives, pursue personal happiness, and ultimately live their dreams. Devising a strategy for moving to the next stage should push business owners to think deeply about what the ultimate meaning of their lives is and how they want to fulfill that meaning.

You don't just have to take our word about the topic. Bruce Wright, a pioneer in the financial planning field, argued persuasively for this approach to business transitions (pivoting from day-to-day management and living for the business to operating the business to live a more complete and fulfilling life). In his book *The Wright Exit Strategy*, Wright pointed out that making a game plan for a shift to another phase of life should ultimately be about defining the purpose of life. "A lot of people will work even when they don't need to work for money or income," he said.[8] "Why? Some people have the perception that if they 'retire,' they won't be doing anything. They don't recognize that they can be actively engaged in doing other things because they have no real purpose in their lives. Their lives have been defined based upon what they did for a living instead of what good they accomplished or what they really could be doing. You must consider what the best use of your time, talents, and resources is. What is the purpose of your life?"

Wright employed this method of combining transition planning and life planning in his work with many of his clients, including one of Intel's founders. To help his clients frame their next phase of their

---

8   Bruce R. Wright, *The Wright Exit Strategy* (SAMMI Press: 1998).

lives, Wright suggested that they ask themselves some questions. A list of some of his most pressing questions follows:

1. If you could wave a magic wand and create the perfect lifestyle or existence for your family, what would it be like?

2. If you could throw away your calendar and replace it with one that took full advantage of your time, talent, and resources, what would it look like?

3. If you could change any list of things in the world, your community, and your country, what would they be?

4. What is preventing or delaying you from doing those things that are the best use of your time, talent, and resources?

5. What is the purpose of money?

We recommend that business owners answer all of these questions to the best of their ability. The process of working through the list makes for an excellent exercise to get owners moving forward. If owners find that they can't fully articulate all of the answers, they should not fret. A good advisor will be able to help them with the tougher questions. The advisor can then assist owners in processing that information and reaching financial goals that are personal to them and not wealth planning industry marketing goals or "if I were you" advice from a third-party perspective.

Wright acknowledged that responding to the questions can be tough for most people.

Even when they get engaged in brainstorming about these and similar questions, he said, getting their significant others to enter the conversation can be challenging. "For some people, it takes a major crisis to move them to act," Wright said. "If your spouse or business partner isn't 'thirsty' enough to do what's best, don't despair. Perhaps you'll just need to exercise them a bit." If partners or significant others are prepared to engage, a good advisor can prove helpful in getting both partners to reach points of clarity.

Daniel Horowitz, a philosopher who has written widely about happiness and money, concurs with Wright's position. Horowitz often reminded his readers of the things that money can't do. "Money can't buy happiness; human beings need social bonds, satisfying work, and strong communities," he said. "A life based entirely on the pursuit of pleasure ultimately becomes pleasure-less."

Lynne Twist, a guru of life planning, is yet another deep thinker who has discussed how challenging it can be for many people to pivot away from making money and toward pursuing personal happiness. In her book *The Soul of Money*, Twist discussed a couple of key concepts to help people make that pivot: the "powerful grip that money has on our lives," and the "immense healing power of even the smallest amount of money when we use it to express our humanity—our highest ideals and our most soulful commitments and values."[9] She worked with some successful and wealthy men who had lost their way. Their lives had become about money and the thrill and accumulation of it. It fed a drive to accumulate money to the detriment of everything else and a mindset of winning by having the most. Living life to its fullest wasn't on their radar. Twist's mission was to reorient their thinking and behavior about the value of wealth. As she stated, "there are hundreds of spiritual practices, many paths that lead people to wholeness and peace of mind." Exploring the relationship with money can lead you to that place. At the very least, it's a wake-up call, so those in this position don't end up in deep emotional pain as age creeps in and the end of life gets closer.

---

9   Lynne Twist, The Soul of Money: Transforming Your Relationship with Money and
     Life (New York, Norton: 2003).

Living Your Dreams

In considering the question of why to engage in full step-by-step holistic planning that incorporates both personal and business goals, business owners—and particularly those who have put off discussions about a change—should take inspiration from Wright, Twist, Horowitz, and others. Owners should give themselves pause to consider how their businesses fit into the bigger picture of their lives—

> *Owners should give themselves pause to consider how their businesses fit into the bigger picture of their lives.*

and the lives of their significant others and families. For most business owners, deliberation on such weighty questions is not easy.

Most business owners' personal experiences are dictated and controlled by what's happening at the business at that moment in time. This is especially true during the initial stages of starting the company, as it is a matter of survival. That laser focus that startup owners place on putting out fires then carries over to the growth stages and eventually gets so ingrained that it becomes the norm. Rather than using the business as a vehicle to reach the owner's personal end-in-mind goals and desires, the business becomes the end game in itself. Of course, engaging in this cycle requires a business owner to sacrifice his personal life with family and friends. They then get lost in the business and the chase to keep it thriving.

But there should come a time when business owners break that cycle, when they step back and shift from an "achievement" mindset to "quality of life" values and concerns. And in that shift, they will inevitably drill down to explore the essential things in their lives.

What are those things that bring them and their significant other the greatest joy and excitement? What are their goals, desires, and objectives, both financial and nonfinancial? Of course, other burning questions emerge: Why is business ownership worth it; what is the ultimate payoff for engaging in the challenges of business ownership; and ultimately, what does it mean to live your dreams? It's about more than just money. It's tough, soul-searching, dare-to-dream reflections to sort out life's purpose and determine when enough is enough.

A potential client once asked us, "What are some of the questions you ask in helping people discover their core values and objectives?" He had this deer-in-the-headlights look as we went through a couple of questions. "I've never thought about those things," he said. Our reply: "Isn't it about time you did?"

We have worked with many clients who have explored the essential questions—including Wright's list and some questions of our own and others. Many have, with coaching and guidance, successfully shifted their mindset about their businesses—and their lives.

Just as we encourage our clients to start addressing key issues concerning their businesses and their lives, we challenge you, too, to kick start the process toward living your dreams. It will only happen when you acknowledge the importance of acting immediately, when you shift from thinking about taking control of your destiny to doing something about it.

There are a number of immediate action items you can do to get engaged in the process. Might it be possible or practical for you to take a week away from the business to gain a sense of how dependent the business is on you and vice versa? If that's feasible, do it. If it seems hard, it's a good sign that you have some work to do to minimize those dependencies. Still, you can and should do a couple of other things that will help you move toward the broader goals we've discussed. Take a break from your usual Saturday afternoon routine and complete our Graduate Level of Business Ownership Workbook, which includes a set of questions and assessments to help you assess and measure your current circumstance and how prepared you are to handle an urgent life altering event. You can find this workbook at www.thegraduatelevelofbusinessownership.com. The results will be a really good start on what improvements need to be made to reduce dependency, increase profitability and business value, and determine what personal planning may be necessary. After performing these exercises, you should be in a good position to meet with an experienced advisor. In any case, you will need an advisor to follow through with the next steps. Finding an advisor you are compatible with can be tough. We have provided a few guidelines about the qualities that make for a good advisor to provide a framework for your search.

Justin is one example of a business owner who began with this exit readiness review and eventually conducted a refocus of his relationship to his business and his life. He's the owner of a thriving electrical components distribution business with several locations across Texas. He started it fifteen years before we met him, after working for a similar business in a different state. The company's revenues reached above $10 million. He had a loyal group of customers, respect in the market, and a good lifestyle. By these and other measures, Justin was successful to anyone who looked at him and the business from the outside.

But a more in-depth view told another story. When Justin approached us, his business had begun to lose revenue. The economic recession of 2008 had hit the company hard.

Business revenues declined, requiring Justin to cut back on staff. At the same time, Justin also felt that he had become shackled to his business. He was convinced that it could not operate without him. He was the first at his desk each morning and the last to leave. Every decision, big or small, had to be run by him. He could never leave. It's almost as if he got onto the hamster wheel, and now he did not know how to get off of it. This dependency proved massively time consuming. Because Justin lacked the expertise of other people to turn to, he also made his share of bad decisions.

On a personal level Justin was also going through a tough phase. He had just gone through a messy divorce, leaving him emotionally stressed. He had partial custody of his two adolescent sons and was juggling his schedule to make time to spend with them. The business issues coupled with personal woes drove Justin into deep introspection. He wondered whether he had the fire to continue with the business or if he should sell it.

Our work advising and coaching Justin had two facets. One was to help him tackle the challenges of the business. The other, perhaps larger focus, was on coaching Justin to rethink his perspective on his role as a business owner and start following a different path. A big part of the work was devoted to balancing his work and his personal life. The process of removing each of the obstacles to his freedom came more slowly. It started by convincing him to take some time off and eventually work his way to a five-week vacation. That was a key step in helping Justin realize that the business could survive without him. That insight, backed by business counseling, led Justin to reframe his understanding of his engagement in the day-to-day operations of the company. With time, Justin started taking Fridays off, spending more time with his kids, enjoying his life and newfound freedoms. Eventually, he embraced having a more limited role in the business while others were running it. He had moved from being a business owner tied down to his business to an investor who could now monitor his assets and manage the team that had taken over much of the day-to-day running of his business.

Most importantly, he saw that this new approach did not diminish the business's success and, at the same time, gave him time and space to enjoy his life.

Although Justin's story is unique, one feature of it is common among the business owners we have advised as they establish a journey toward success. They have all started by working at, and eventually gaining, a different vision of their businesses and their lives. Once owners have established and articulated where they want to go in life, that narrative should then be the driver for all their business strategies going forward. The business then becomes the vehicle for owners to obtain their ultimate objectives.

The Time to Act Is Now— You Have the Power

Grasping the interconnection between operating the business, life planning, pursuing happiness, transition planning, and potential exit planning makes it easy for business owners to realize when they should begin the process of phasing out of the day-to-day responsibility of running the business. It should be clear that owners shouldn't wait. They should not let the long list of reasons and rationalizations often used keep them from starting. When weighed against the urgent need to get busy doing the things they want, things that will bring greater enjoyment and fulfillment, excuses for putting things off ring hollow.

Most business owners, in our experience, have 70 to 95 percent of their wealth tied up in their business. As an owner, you need to know that you have the power to control the annual amount you take out of the business. You have the power to grow the business's value to an amount you've identified to let you live your desired lifestyle when you choose to monetize. You have the power to ensure you reach all of your top personal goals and objectives. You have the power to decide when you exit, to whom you sell/transfer, and how much you exit the business with. Many business owners we have come across had been reluctant to make that leap, to use that power effectively. But after starting the process with us, they saw the positive results in very short order. They understood very quickly how much they could do with proper guidance to control their own destiny.

It is our hope that the stories, information, advice, and insights in this book get you thinking about looking at your business and personal life in a totally different perspective. The stakes are high, and you have the power to make what could be one of the most positive consequential decisions in your and your family's life. All it takes is taking that first all-important step. Be bold! Step out of the ordinary! Similar to professional athletics, having a coach to guide, encourage, and push you will keep you on track to reach your stated goals. Meet with an experienced business advisor. Explore the possibilities. Like the many clients we've worked with, you and your family will be glad you did. Good luck!

ABOUT THE AUTHORS

RONEN SHEFER is a founding partner of ROCG Americas and has served as the managing partner since its inception in 2004. Ronen has been instrumental to the development of ROCG in North America, the growth of its brand, and the implementation of its key strategic initiatives. Ronen is also a member of ROCG's executive committee, which manages ROCG's global initiatives.

Born and raised in Israel, Ronen moved to the United States when he was in his early twenties. While starting his career as a CPA, Ronen recognized early on that business owners were seeking a level of advice they were not getting from the profession at the time. Business owners no longer wanted accountants to simply be scorekeepers, they needed help with their current business challenges, and they wanted someone who is willing to take the journey alongside them. That observation was the beginning of a mission that started with a simple principal in mind, that "every client we take on is a business we lose sleep on, just like their owners."

As a result, and for almost three decades, Ronen has specialized in guiding entrepreneurs and business owners through their unique challenges of owning their businesses and toward the graduate level of business ownership. Ronen continues to believe that each client is unique and that, nowadays, they not only require business advisory and planning, but they also need someone to help oversee the successful implementation of these plans in a manner that fits their unique circumstances.

When he is not working with clients, you can frequently find Ronen speaking throughout the country on business growth strategies and successful exit planning. He has authored several articles in business publications covering common business ownership challenges. Finally, Ronen is also known to volunteer his time to assist small businesses and startups with their planning process, including serving on their advisory boards from time to time.

TERENCE (TERRY) J. SHEPHERD is a founding partner of the consulting company ROCG. He is also a managing partner of S&G LLP, a business consulting and CPA firm, cofounded with Carl Goldstein in 1980, with two offices located in Massachusetts. Terry is a CPA, has a master's of science degree in taxation (MST), and is a Certified Merger and Acquisition Advisor (CM&AA). He has advised small- and medium-sized, family-owned and closely held businesses for over forty years.

His areas of expertise are in value growth and strategic planning and execution, business exit and transition planning and execution, family business planning, M&A advisory, business strategic tax planning, personal life/estate planning, and individual tax planning.

In Terry's business transition consulting work, he is a catalyst in guiding owners to discover their personal values, goals, and objectives to ensure that they're aligned with and can be met while running their business, enabling them to lead a more fulfilling and enjoyable life. Terry is especially skilled in understanding the emotional right-brain attributes involved with family businesses, business owners transitioning through each growth cycle, and an owner's eventual exit from the business, either through a sale to an outside party or a next generation transfer.

Terry is a frequent speaker at business seminars regarding building business value, profitability, strategic planning, and business transition and exit planning. He has spoken throughout the country at trade shows, chambers of commerce, business publication events, and at ROCG events. He has also authored many articles for many different publications and was the principal writer in ROCG's white paper, "Business Transition/Succession: The Increased Risk of Incurring Catastrophic Losses and What You Can Do About It."